T0026413

SALES 101

FROM **FINDING LEADS** AND **CLOSING TECHNIQUES** TO **RETAINING CUSTOMERS** AND **GROWING YOUR BUSINESS,** AN ESSENTIAL PRIMER ON **HOW TO SELL**

WENDY CONNICK

Adams Media

New York   London   Toronto   Sydney   New Delhi

DEDICATION

For my mother, because she's the best.

Adams Media
An Imprint of Simon & Schuster, Inc.
100 Technology Center Drive
Stoughton, Massachusetts 02072

First Adams Media hardcover edition September 2019

ADAMS MEDIA and colophon are trademarks of Simon & Schuster.

For information about special discounts for bulk purchases, please contact Simon & Schuster Special Sales at 1-866-506-1949 or business@simonandschuster.com.

The Simon & Schuster Speakers Bureau can bring authors to your live event. For more information or to book an event contact the Simon & Schuster Speakers Bureau at 1-866-248-3049 or visit our website at www.simonspeakers.com.

Manufactured in the United States of America

2 2022

Library of Congress Cataloging-in-Publication Data
Names: Connick, Wendy, author.
Title: Sales 101 / Wendy Connick.
Description: Avon, Massachusetts: Adams Media, 2019.
Series: Adams 101.
Includes index.
Identifiers: LCCN 2019015817 | ISBN 9781507211038 (hc) | ISBN 9781507211045 (ebook)
Subjects: LCSH: Selling. | Home-based businesses. | BISAC: BUSINESS & ECONOMICS / Sales & Selling. | BUSINESS & ECONOMICS / Home-Based Businesses.
Classification: LCC HF5438.25 .C65365 2019 | DDC 658.85--dc23

LC record available at https://lccn.loc.gov/2019015817

ISBN 978-1-5072-1103-8
ISBN 978-1-5072-1104-5 (ebook)

CONTENTS

INTRODUCTION

Like every other aspect of business these days, sales is changing. In today's highly competitive marketplace, with the addition of high-speed communication, social media, and volatile economic conditions, skilled, successful salespeople are in high demand.

Sales 101 walks you through the sales process in clear, straightforward entries. Perhaps you're new to the profession or are just thinking about getting into it. Maybe you've been doing it for years or need to integrate sales techniques into your current role. Whatever your relationship to sales, this book will offer you useful tips showing you how to get better at it.

At its core, sales is about forging positive connections with other people. Good salespeople accomplish this by turning their own personalities into an asset. That's why different salespeople use such different approaches to selling. The trick is to find the sales tactics that mesh well with your own personality traits; these are the tactics that will let you be yourself with prospects and customers. Being a good salesperson is about teamwork. It's about finding the right approach to the product or service you're selling and overcoming customer objections and barriers. You have to focus on your company's goals, keeping in mind that an extremely successful month doesn't give you the right to rest on your laurels the following month.

This book will provide you with a thorough grounding in the basic details you need to be a good salesperson—from shaping your presentation to cold calling to networking. Throughout, you'll find dozens of examples to show you what to emulate and what to avoid.

As you work your way through this book, you'll be able to take the basic tips and tricks provided here and adapt them for your own preferences and situation. These ideas are the building blocks you need to craft the perfect scripts, presentations, emails, and everything else required to succeed as a salesperson.

It's all here in *Sales 101*. Let's get going!

CHAPTER 1
SALES BASICS

If you're interested in going into sales, you need to master some learned skills and will continue to polish and improve on them throughout your career. You'll need to make some preparations before you even land a sales job to help your first days and weeks go smoothly. All salespeople must understand the steps that go into each sale—from finding leads all the way to asking for referrals. Mastering the sales cycle allows you to keep prospects moving smoothly through your pipeline and helps you to figure out what to do when a sale goes drastically wrong.

IS SALES RIGHT FOR YOU?

What a Sales Job Is Really Like

The stereotypical salesperson is a smooth talker, is sociable, and can convince anyone of anything. In reality, that kind of salesperson rarely becomes a star performer. As one veteran sales manager put it, "Salespeople have one mouth and two ears because you're supposed to use your ears twice as often as your mouth."

The following traits are the ones that truly matter if you want to be a good (or better yet, great) salesperson.

INTEGRITY

Integrity is important for all professionals, but it's doubly important for salespeople. Because salespeople have an unfortunate reputation for shading the truth and otherwise acting unethically, you'll need to take special pains to keep your behavior above reproach.

Being a person of high integrity means acting both morally and ethically. *Morality* means choosing to do what's right based on an internal code of honor; *ethics* means obeying the rules set down by other authorities, including your employer. Good salespeople need to adhere to both sets of guidelines.

When there's a conflict between your morals and ethics, or if you're otherwise not sure of the right thing to do, turn to the guiding principle for sales: always put the customer's needs first.

Good salespeople don't try to trick people into buying something that's not the best product or service for them. They help prospective customers identify their most important needs and find a product that will meet those needs.

As a salesperson, you represent the company you work for. Part of your job is helping your company build and maintain a good reputation through your actions. Sales is just as much a service job as medicine or police work—if you think of your field in that light, you'll have an easier time putting integrity first.

EMPATHY

Empathy is the ability to understand and share other people's feelings. As a salesperson, you'll talk to dozens or even hundreds of other people every day. Good salespeople know that they can make every one of these contacts a positive experience for the other person. Empathy is the cornerstone for positive communication: it allows you to guide the conversation in ways that benefit the other party.

Empathic salespeople listen carefully and use open-ended questions to uncover prospect and customer needs. They can relate to people from all walks of life and communicate in ways that make others feel comfortable and safe. They truly care about helping other people, so they get great satisfaction from finding just the right product or service that will make the customer's problem go away.

Empathy will not only allow you to do your job well; it also will help you to enjoy it. If you feel great about what you do because you love helping other people, you'll be both a happier person and a more effective salesperson.

TENACITY

Sales is hard work. Many prospects are so hardened to salespeople that their reply to anything you say is an automatic "No, thanks." It takes time, energy, and commitment to break through that wall and earn such a prospect's trust. One important part of this is building up touchpoints.

A touchpoint is a point of contact between a seller (i.e., your company) and a prospective buyer. As a salesperson, you'll create touchpoints every time you communicate in any way with prospects or customers—even when that communication is as impersonal as posting on social media. However, it can take dozens or even hundreds of touchpoints to nudge a particular prospect into buying something.

Touchpoints

A touchpoint can be as simple as seeing an ad on TV or visiting a company's website. Sales touchpoints are among the most interactive and occur at a particularly important point in the buying cycle, so they're often pivotal.

Tenacious salespeople don't give up when the first few touchpoints fail to move a prospect; they make a note in the prospect's record to reach out to them a few weeks later and move on to the next prospect.

When things are going badly and you're struggling to close a sale—any sale—tenacity will be what helps you get through the slump without falling apart. Tenacity can also help you with internal interactions. For example, if you're trying to convince your sales manager that your quota is unrealistically high, it will probably take more than one attempt to bring her around. Tenacity helps you to keep trying until you either get what you want or at least manage a compromise.

BASIC SALES SKILLS

The Salesperson's Must-Have Qualities

If you've got all the important traits mentioned in the previous section, then you've got what you need to get you to the starting line. However, to become a good salesperson, you'll also need to acquire certain learned skills.

COMMUNICATION

Salespeople spend most of their time talking to other people: prospects, customers, employees from other departments, their managers, and miscellaneous others. These conversations typically involve trying to convince the other party to do something. That means you'll need to be a skilled communicator to do your job well.

Communication doesn't just cover the times when you're the one doing the communicating; it also means being a good *listener*. Good communicators know how to draw out other people. They ask questions that get people talking, pick out the important details they need from what they hear, and use those details to create a compelling argument.

Being an excellent listener is actually more important and useful for sales than being an excellent talker. With experience, you'll find that if you can get a prospect to speak freely, he'll often talk himself right into buying from you.

EXPERTISE

Successful salespeople are experts in the fields related to the products and services they sell. Remember, your job as a salesperson is to match up prospective customers with the products that will solve their problems. You can't do that well if you don't understand both the products you sell and the problems that your customers face on a regular basis.

Product knowledge is the first and most basic level of expertise that salespeople must acquire. Before you can sell effectively, you'll need to know your products backward and forward. That doesn't just mean reading user manuals, although that's a good place to start. If possible, you should use the products you sell yourself—as often as you can manage it. If that's not an option, at least attend a demo or watch someone else using the product. Your company probably releases new products and services on a regular basis, so acquiring product knowledge is an ongoing process.

The second part of sales expertise is understanding your customers. If you sell to other businesses in a particular industry, you should know that industry backward and forward. Read trade journals, lurk on social media boards related to that industry, and attend relevant trade shows and webinars.

If you sell to a specific subset of consumers, learn everything you can about that subset and the concerns that bring them to you. For example, if you sell baby clothes, study parenting, newborn care, and baby fashion.

Finally, if you sell to a broader audience of businesses or consumers, learn all you can about the particular issue that your products address and about the alternate ways to resolve that issue. For example, if you sell smartphones, you'll need to learn how smartphones differ from basic cell phones and tablets, why people choose smart-phones over the other options, and how your company's phones compare to the competitors'.

TEAMWORK

Good salespeople are able to get along and work well with others. In a good-sized company each department consists of three types of employees: a few people who are really good at their jobs, a few who are flat-out terrible, and a number of reasonably competent employees who make up the rest of the group. As a salesperson, you must figure out where your coworkers fit in that system, especially for departments that are likely to interact with your customers.

Once you've identified the employees you can trust to do a great job, the next step is to get on good terms with those employees. Good relationships with your most talented coworkers can help you solve any number of problems: engineering department employees will walk you through how a new product works, shipping department employees can help you by expediting deliveries for anxious customers, marketing department employees will work with you to find relevant leads, and so on.

Good teamwork isn't limited to your coworkers; it also includes your customers and your professional contacts outside your company. Good relationships with customers will help you keep them loyal for life, will result in numerous referrals, and will turn them into company ambassadors. And good relationships with professional contacts will help you build a strong and flourishing network that will make just about every aspect of your work easier, from finding a sales job in the first place to helping you reach an elusive prospect.

ACQUIRING SALES SKILLS

In a perfect world your company would provide all the sales training you need. In reality most salespeople have to take responsibility for their own career development.

Webinars

Many companies and institutions hold free webinars to teach various sales skills. Do a quick search online for the skill you want to perfect plus the word *webinar*, and you may find just what you need.

Try to set aside a portion of every workday to read some useful sales-related material. The time can be a mere fifteen minutes per day, and the material can be sales books, blogs, websites, or social media sites—as long as they have something new that you can apply to your job. When you stumble upon an interesting tip or idea, write it down. You can sort these ideas into two lists: one for tips that you want to start using right away, and another for ideas that you can't implement yet but will try in the future.

Other salespeople can be a great source for sales knowledge and techniques. If you're fairly new to sales, then you'll definitely want to learn from your team's experienced members. Ask one or two of the best salespeople on your team if you can listen in on their cold calls and/or come with them on appointments, and then take plenty of notes. If you're a more experienced salesperson yourself, you can exchange ideas with other salespeople on your team. You might even set up a group that meets regularly for that purpose.

BEFORE YOU START SELLING

Prepping for Your First Sales Job

The first step toward becoming a salesperson is finding and getting hired for a sales job. Once you've managed that feat, you'll have a lot to learn during your first days and weeks on the job.

THE SALES RESUME

Good resumes share certain attributes regardless of the type of job, but sales resumes require a few special tweaks.

First, put your major accomplishments right at the top of the resume. Sales managers often spend only a few seconds skimming each resume, so you want to ensure that they will see your most enticing points. These accomplishments should be as specific as possible. For example, instead of writing "Top customer service representative at Company X," write "Ranked top customer service representative at Company X three years in a row." Use specific numbers whenever possible.

Breaking Into Sales

The first sales job is often the most challenging to find, because you don't have much relevant experience. A multi-level marketing (MLM) program, such as Amway or Mary Kay, can be a fast way to get some sales experience for your resume.

You should also mention any useful connections you have, relating to either sales in general or the specific industry your target employer sells to. Because relationships are so important in sales, being able to bring a ton of important contacts with you is a big selling point to a prospective employer. If you have impressive social media statistics, like a huge network on *LinkedIn* with connections inside major companies, list those as well.

After you've listed your accomplishments at the top of your resume, it's time to break down your career history. Talk about how your work benefited the company and its customers. Again, use specific numbers whenever you can. Mention things like the awards you received and the major clients you helped bring on board or kept from churning (moving on to a competitor).

Next comes the section detailing your training and education. List any degrees you have as well as any job-specific courses you've completed. Don't forget certifications! They're especially helpful if they relate to your intended employer's industry (i.e., computer networking certifications for a company that sells products to network engineers).

Each time you apply for a job, you'll need to customize your basic sales resume to fit the new opening. Add a sentence at the top describing why you're applying for this job and how you can benefit the company. Ideally, you should also tweak the rest of your resume to play to those strengths that will be particularly applicable to the prospective employer.

Before you send off your resume, check your contacts to see if they include anyone who works for the company in question. If you find one, give that person a call and ask for advice. She may know something about the position or the company that isn't public knowledge and that you can work into your resume or reference during the interview.

FINDING THE RIGHT SALES JOB

Because great salespeople are relatively rare, you're likely to see sales positions posted on job boards and the like no matter what the economy is doing. But not all of those sales jobs are likely to be a good fit for you. Before you start applying, you'll need to do a little legwork.

First, consider which job attributes are most important to you. Do you like working closely with a sales team, or do you prefer independence? Do you like to have a base salary, or do you enjoy the challenge of pure commissions? Is telecommuting a big plus for you? Are there specific industries or types of customers you prefer? Make a list with the most important factors at the top, and keep this list in front of you as you peruse the assorted job postings. If you really need a job *now*, you may need to compromise on some of these factors, but you will usually be able to find a few jobs that match at least one or two of your top priorities.

Once you've identified a likely position, start digging into the company's background—and you'll want to do a deeper dive than just glancing through the corporate website. Sites like *Glassdoor* can get you the inside scoop on what a company is really like.

Once you've started sending out applications and getting responses, try to arrange the interview schedule so that your interviews for less desirable jobs come first. That gives you a chance to polish your presentation and try out some answers to common interview questions.

YOUR FIRST DAY AS A SALESPERSON

Even for an experienced salesperson, starting a job with a new company means learning quite a few new things: from the product to the sales cycle to the corporate culture to the other team members and more. As a brand-new salesperson at a new company, you've got even more to learn. The good news is that your coworkers can provide the resources you need to get off to a good start.

Get to know as many of your fellow salespeople as possible, particularly the superstar performers. Take the top salesperson out to lunch or to the nearest coffee shop and pump her for information. Odds are she will be flattered by the attention (and the free food) and will be happy to help. If possible, ask to spend an hour listening to her phone calls or go along on the next round of appointments. Take copious notes to use as a basis for writing your own pitches.

Your non-sales coworkers can help you master the products and services you'll be selling. If your company has a customer service department, make friends there and ask them to fill you in about the products. Get familiar with the company's promotional items (brochures, white papers, websites, etc.). Once you've mastered the product features, make a list of possible benefits for each. Here are a few of the many benefits your products might offer:

- Convenience
- Security
- Efficiency
- Financial value
- Ease of use
- Prestige

Work these benefits into sentences, like, "This channel package *saves you money* by giving you the *most prestigious* sports channel at a discount."

Finally, your new manager can help you with basic information, like where to get copies of brochures and other marketing materials, your sales goals and priorities, the equipment you'll be using and its nuances, and so on.

THE SEVEN-STAGE SALES CYCLE

From Prospecting to Referrals

Every sale follows roughly the same seven-step cycle. If you want to do well in sales, you'll need to master each one of these stages.

PROSPECTING FOR LEADS

Leads are consumers or businesses that may be potential customers. Finding leads is the first stage of the sales cycle, and it's a critical one. A sales pipeline is actually shaped more like a funnel than a pipe: it's widest at the beginning of the sales process because you'll lose a percentage of your prospects during each stage of the sales cycle. By the time you reach the last stage, you will likely have only a small fraction left of the initial group of prospects. So if you don't come up with significant numbers of leads, you'll be awfully short on potential customers by the end of the sales process.

What Is a Sales Pipeline?

A sales pipeline is a way of breaking down your leads and prospects based on where they are in the sales cycle. Customer relationship management (CRM) software often classifies records by their stage in the pipeline.

SET AN APPOINTMENT

The most common rookie salesperson mistake is trying to sell your product as soon as you reach a potential customer. At that point in the relationship your prospects are not going to be ready to consider buying from you. When you pick up the phone and start calling leads, or walk into a neighborhood and start knocking on doors, the goal should almost always be to get an appointment with a decision-maker. Once you're at the actual appointment, you can start pitching the product. But in your initial conversation the only thing you should be pitching is an appointment.

QUALIFY THE PROSPECT

Qualifying is the process that allows you to find out whether a lead is actually a prospect. This usually takes the form of asking predetermined questions designed to identify the qualities that any prospect will have. Many salespeople ask a few prequalifying questions before setting an appointment, but the bulk of the qualification process happens at the appointment. How and when you decide to qualify prospects will be up to you; there's a balance you'll need to find between asking too many questions early and driving away the prospect, and not asking enough questions and wasting time with non-prospects.

MAKE YOUR PRESENTATION

You've spent hours placing cold calls and have managed to book a few appointments during which you'll have a chance to make your sales presentation. How you act during your presentation will determine whether you'll get the sale or walk away in defeat. Your goal during a sales presentation is to prove to your prospect that the product or service you're offering will solve an important problem for her. The traditional sales presentation, where the salesperson talks on and on about the product and the prospect just sits there, isn't the best way to sell. Interactive presentations are much more effective, since they keep your prospects engaged and interested.

ADDRESS OBJECTIONS

In sales, an objection is a concern that the prospect raises about buying something. An objection can be a sign that the prospect is interested, that he wants more information, that he's concerned about something, that he doesn't trust you, that he is not at all interested and wants to get rid of you without an argument, or a combination of several of these things. In other words, there may be a lot more going on than whatever issue the prospect has raised. To continue on to the next stage of the sales cycle, you'll need to handle not only the objection itself but also whatever else may be behind it.

CLOSE THE SALE

Closing is the moment when you openly ask the prospect to make the purchase. If during your presentation you did a good job of convincing the prospect that he needs what you have to sell, then closing the sale will follow naturally. However, even the most interested prospect won't close himself. You'll need to provide at least a small nudge to get the sale closed—and if the prospect isn't fully convinced yet, closing may require more than a nudge from you. When a prospect pushes back with more objections, you'll need to step back and figure out where you went wrong. In some cases, when you just can't get a particularly tough prospect to make a decision, you'll want to haul out one of the tried-and-true closing techniques to seal the deal.

ASK FOR REFERRALS

Referrals—warm leads to new prospects—are invaluable to salespeople. It's typically much easier to close a sale with a referral than it is to close one with a cold lead. Just after you've closed someone is the best time to get referrals from them, because they're excited about their new purchase, yet many salespeople are so relieved to get a sale from someone that they race out the door without even asking for referrals. If you take the time to ask every new customer for at least one referral, you'll soon find you don't need to make as many cold calls—a realization that just about every salesperson will greet with joy.

CHAPTER 2
PROSPECTING

The word *prospecting* raises mental images of miners crouched over a muddy stream, panning for gold. This is actually not far from how salespeople use the term, but instead of panning for gold nuggets, you're looking for the people who will become your future customers. To be a successful prospector, you must know where to look for leads, how to sort out the ones who have the potential to buy from you (a.k.a. prospects), and how to identify the most promising prospects for extra attention. Setting up your own small-scale lead generation campaigns can help immensely, as these campaigns bring you prequalified leads who are already eager to learn more. Finally, once you've started collecting leads, you'll need a system to manage them and keep them organized.

BEFORE YOU START PROSPECTING

Setting Up a System

Prospecting is the first step in the sales cycle, so all the other stages depend upon it. Before you can successfully prospect for leads, you must understand what a "good" lead looks like for the product or service you're selling.

Marketing professionals create what they call buyer personas to help them target their campaigns. Ask your marketing department to provide you with copies of any buyer personas they've created. If they don't have personas for you, you'll need to create something similar that you can use to figure out what a "good" lead might look like.

Buyer Personas

A buyer persona is a fictional representation of a desirable type of customer. These personas incorporate market research data into a "character" description, like something you'd find in a movie script. Salespeople don't have to go into this much detail when creating personas, but you should use similar information.

First, pull up your records of existing customers and look for your favorites—the customers who regularly and loyally purchase from the company. Compare those records to each other and see what these particular customers have in common. That may include demographic information such as income level, family size, location, hobbies, major purchases (for example, do they own their own home?), education level, and so on.

Once you've identified these commonalities, you can focus your search on leads who share those qualities. If your company provides you with lead lists, you can use this information to prioritize the lists so you can focus on the most promising leads. If you do your own lead generation, these demographic details will help you figure out where to look.

The next step in pre-prospecting planning is to figure out just how many leads you need in order to end up with enough sales to hit your quota. If you don't put enough time into prospecting and fail to uncover enough solid leads, you won't be able to make enough sales. On the other hand, if you spend too much time on prospecting, you'll be splitting your efforts between too many different leads and won't be able to give each one the attention it requires.

That's why a wise salesperson does some basic forecasting before she starts prospecting. No forecasting method is 100 percent accurate, but there's a simple method that will give you a good idea of how many new leads you'll need in the near future.

First, list any prospects currently in your pipeline. It's better to enter this data in a word processing or spreadsheet program to simplify the modifications you will be making to the list in the future. You'll want four columns in your list: the name of the prospect, the expected value of the sale, the probability of closing the sale, and the value you expect to get from the sale.

The column with the expected value should reflect your estimate of how much revenue you'll be generating from the sale. For example, if a prospect is interested in a product priced at $500 but you expect to convince him to add a maintenance plan that costs $50 more, you would enter an expected value for that prospect of $550. It's harder to estimate the likelihood that the sale will close. More often than not, though, you'll have a reasonable sense of where a specific sale stands at a given point in the cycle. If you are really not sure, ask for feedback from the prospect. Even if they don't give you an honest answer, you can at least get a sense of where you stand. The information entered in this column should express the likelihood (as a percentage) of closing the sale. As an example, if you believe the odds of closing the sale are fifty-fifty, enter 50 percent in this column.

After you enter the data in the four columns, multiply the expected value by the probability percentage to calculate the value you think the sale will generate. This is the amount that goes into the fourth column. This amount won't be the same as the actual sale amount for an individual sale, as you'll either close the deal and make more money or not close it and make nothing at all. However, the amount of all the individual items for every transaction in your pipeline ought to be close to your actual sales income from the prospects in your current pipeline.

To make your projections even more accurate, create a timetable for them by making an additional chart, with the name of the prospect in the left column and additional columns for each upcoming month. Enter the projected total value in the column for the month when you anticipate the transaction will probably close. For example, if you are entering the data in March and you think it will probably close in a month, enter the projected total value of the sale in the column for April. When the timetable is complete, you can total the amount in the column for each month to provide you with an approximate revenue estimate you expect to produce for that month.

You should update your charts weekly or even more often as you develop more prospects and move existing prospects through the sales cycle. You will find it is worth devoting a few minutes each day to have a much more accurate sense of the value of what's in your pipeline and whether to increase the amount of prospecting you do to increase your sales. This will make it easier to keep your sales results consistent and prevent unexpected dips from month to month.

FINDING LEADS

Where to Look for the Best Opportunities

It's great when you can get all the leads you need from lists that your employer provides. But even if you have access to lead lists, there will probably be times when you run through all your available leads and still feel the need for more prospects. In that case you can try one of these approaches to rustle up some new leads for your pipeline.

DIRECTORIES

Directories aren't limited to resources like Internet reverse lookups and the Yellow Pages—although those tools can certainly be helpful. Many companies make it their business to organize information on both companies and consumers, using it to create huge databases. These databases typically require a paid subscription, but your local library may be able to provide free access.

Time versus Money

Sourcing leads generally requires an investment of either time or money. For example, buying a pre-generated lead list will cost you money, while combing through directories will cost you time. Either approach can work, so you'll need to decide which you value more: your time or your money.

Most hard-copy business directories will be located in the reference section, so ask your reference librarian which ones they carry and where to find them. If your local library doesn't have the directories you need, then placing a request with the librarian might be enough to get the library to subscribe. Most libraries have computers that patrons can use to go online, and the librarian will be able to give you sign-in details for the relevant directory services websites. Prestigious directory services include InfoUSA, D&B Hoovers, Standard and Poor's, and Salesgenie.

LEAD-RICH LOCATIONS

By this point you should already have a good idea of what your ideal customer looks like. The best leads for you are leads who look as much like your ideal customer as possible. The best place to find those leads is someplace where your ideal customer would choose to go. This could mean trade shows and other such events, but you can also consider places not directly related to sales where you might meet such leads.

For example, is your ideal customer likely to own his own home? If so, try attending events that target homeowners. If you typically sell to technical people, such as engineers or programmers, visit places that appeal to techies—not just trade shows but also events like fairs hosted by computer manufacturers, which would appeal to the technically minded.

GENERAL-PURPOSE LISTINGS

Generally speaking, the more specific a lead list is, the harder and more expensive it will be to acquire that list. You can save some money by starting with a more general version of the lead list you really want, and use e-newsletters and similar approaches to winnow out the leads who are not a good fit for you.

For example, if your ideal customer is someone who owns a midsize manufacturing business and leases his equipment, you can start with a list of midsize manufacturing businesses, and then send emails that will appeal to the ones who lease their equipment. Another approach would be to send a brief survey that includes a question about whether or not the recipient leases his equipment. Whichever approach you use, the replies you get will identify the leads that you want to pursue further.

ADVERTISEMENTS

These days there's a magazine (both print and online) for every possible subject. And the more obscure the subject, the cheaper the ad space. An even more budget-minded option is to use a classified ad in a trade magazine or newspaper. Find two or three publications that your ideal customer would be likely to read, and use them as a way to get in touch. Don't forget to include an offer in your ad that will motivate leads to reach out to you.

SEMINARS

Since your product is designed to solve an important problem for your ideal customer, and since you're hopefully an expert on your product, you have knowledge and resources that can be very useful for people facing that problem. Set up a free seminar in which you will offer suggestions and advice on a subject that would be very interesting to your ideal customer. The people who are likely to attend such a seminar will also be excellent leads for you. And this is a great way to make a strong first impression with them, because your seminar will demonstrate both your expertise and your desire to help them.

OTHER SALESPEOPLE

There are undoubtedly a lot of other salespeople looking for the same kinds of leads that you are. Some of those salespeople are your competitors, but many will be in a related but noncompetitive industry. For example, if you sell mortgages, look for realtors to partner with. The two of you can share leads, essentially giving each of you twice as many leads as you would have alone.

ASSESSING LEADS

How to Tell Whales from Losers

Not all leads are truly prospects, and it behooves you to identify the non-prospects as early as possible. For that matter, not all prospects are equally valuable; some will take incredible effort on your part to close and will never buy more than once, while others will quickly and easily convert to customers and buy new products from you on a regular basis. A good lead qualification system will help you identify both non-prospects and exceptionally good prospects.

The earlier in the sales process you can qualify a lead, the less time you'll end up wasting on non-prospects. On the other hand, peppering a lead with questions before you've even begun to establish a relationship can be a big turnoff.

Many salespeople balance these two concerns by doing a quick prequalification during the initial contact, followed by a more thorough qualification on the second or third contact. If you take a look at your current customers and products, you should be able to come up with a few quick questions that will eliminate most non-prospects. Those can be your prequalification questions.

When you get a bit further along in the sales process, you can ask more questions that will eliminate other non-prospects and will also allow you to sort your prospects into more desirable and less desirable groups.

Before you can start classifying prospects, you'll need to know what a "good" prospect looks like. Regardless of what you're selling, a good prospect is someone who will buy fairly quickly and who will make more than a minimal purchase from you.

The buyer persona you created or borrowed from your company's marketing department is a good place to start, but you'll likely want to narrow down the field further. For instance, if you sell business to business (B2B), you might add that a good prospect is one with a single point of contact with clear buying authority.

How you define "buy fairly quickly" and "minimal purchase" will also depend on your type of selling. If you're selling big-ticket items with complex requirements, a yearlong sales cycle might actually be quite short by your standards. Similarly, a minimal purchase could range from a few dollars to millions. You'll need to look at your past sales to set your own standards for selling cycle time and size of purchase.

Doing a little research on a lead before you ever pick up the phone can bolster your sales efforts immensely. First, this often enables you to immediately cross off unqualified leads without even having to speak with them. Second, you can collect that all-important information about highly qualified leads that will help you to get an appointment.

Cold Call Reluctance

Many salespeople dread cold calling; it's not easy reaching out to people who reject and even abuse you. Cold call reluctance is when a salesperson finds ways to put off cold calling, often to the point where he's barely doing any calling at all.

On the other hand, it's possible to take your research too far. This can happen as a symptom of cold call reluctance—you spend more and more time on the Internet researching your leads, in order to delay the moment when you have to actually talk with someone. But excessive research can also happen because you don't know where to draw the line. There is definitely a point where you're doing so much research that what you uncover won't be worth the time you spent on it.

So how much research is appropriate? There's no one answer to that question, because your research needs will vary according to your customer type, your industry, the types of products and services you're selling, and your own sales approach.

Generally speaking, you'll want to do at least enough research to confirm that the lead is a prospect before you pick up the phone. Checking on these factors usually takes only a few minutes, and it's worth it to avoid calling any non-prospect leads.

Next, you can start checking leads against the characteristics that your best customers tend to share. Researching those particular traits can give you an idea of just how good this lead may be. A lead that matches many of your favorite customer traits is worth a lot more of your time and energy.

DO YOUR RESEARCH

When you're calling B2B leads, it's worth doing a little extra research to uncover more specific contact information. For example, if all you've got is the company's name, look at the company's website and see if you can track down the decision-maker's name and title. Even better, if you can uncover the decision-maker's extension you may be able to avoid getting stalled by a gatekeeper.

Highly qualified leads may be worth a little extra research time to dig up the information you need to make a terrific impression during the sales presentation. For business-to-business (B2B) prospects, that usually includes basic information about the company: what kind of products they make, how well they're doing, if there have been any recent problems or successes of note, what the prospect's customers are saying about them, important events related to the prospect's industry, and so on. For business-to-consumer (B2C) prospects, it might mean scanning the prospect's social media accounts to get a better idea of her personality and what's important to her.

Gatekeepers

A gatekeeper is the person who controls access to a decision-maker. For example, most executives have an assistant whose job is to keep the executive from being bothered by people like you. Getting past gatekeepers can be a challenge, but you'll learn some strategies in Chapter 3 that can help.

Not every lead will be worth this much time and effort. In fact, some salespeople might want to do only the bare minimum of research on *every* lead. For example, if you tend to make high volumes of small sales, then it's not worth spending a lot of time on research for any given prospect.

Finally, when you qualify a lead into a prospect but can't convince him to make a sales appointment, don't give up on him. There are dozens of reasons why a prospect may not be ready to buy when you first speak with him, most of which have nothing to do with you or your product. That's why it's important to keep on nurturing leads even if they're not interested in buying right away. A month or two from now you might call up one of those prospects and discover he's now eager to buy from you. If you give up too easily, you'll miss out on a lot of potential sales—and that will make your job much harder.

LEAD GENERATION TECHNIQUES

How to Attract Sales Leads

Lead generation is the process of attracting leads and convincing them to contact you. It's extremely beneficial for salespeople for two reasons: First, if leads are coming to *you*, you'll have far less cold calling to do, which will save you considerable time and effort. Second, the leads you get through lead generation will be prequalified simply by the fact that they're interested enough to make the effort of reaching out.

Isn't Lead Generation a Marketing Thing?

In most companies lead generation is the marketing department's responsibility. In fact, lead generation is the source of those lead lists your sales manager hands out. However, doing solo lead generation can produce substantial benefits because you can design your program to find precisely the right leads.

Developing a solo lead generation campaign will likely take a fair amount of effort the first time around, but the good news is that you'll be able to use your first campaign as a template for future efforts. As you learn which approaches are most effective, you'll be able to build better campaigns with a minimum of extra work.

INCLUDE THE BASIC ELEMENTS FOR SUCCESS

Creating a marketing campaign, be it for lead generation or some other purpose, can be difficult, but it's not complicated. There are certain components every lead generation campaign should include:

- **A place for leads to sign up to be contacted by you.** This is most often a website, but salespeople can also use low-tech methods. For example, you could leave out a bowl where people can drop their business cards.
- **A way to organize leads.** Customer relationship management (CRM) systems are best for this, but a spreadsheet or even a plain old file folder will do just fine.
- **A plan of action.** You need to know how you'll reach out to potential leads, where to look for them, what kinds of leads you're looking for, and what you'll do once you get them. You should also have a set of goals (how else will you know if your campaign succeeded?) and a time line.
- **An offer.** This is the incentive that you dangle in front of the leads to get them to hand over their contact information. Offers need to be compelling enough to galvanize leads into responding.

An astonishing number of companies launch massive campaigns that don't include one or more of these elements. For example, a quick glance through other companies' lead generation campaigns will probably turn up several that don't include an offer at all, let alone a compelling one. As long as you remember to incorporate all these basic elements, you'll be doing better than many *Fortune* 500 marketing professionals.

HAVE A REALISTIC TIME FRAME

Lead generation of any kind doesn't produce immediate results. That's one reason why it's important for salespeople to keep on prospecting even when they have tons of sales right now—the leads you reach today will become next month's or even next year's sales.

It's important to give any lead generation campaign enough time to work. The exact length of time you'll need will vary depending on what you're selling and who you're selling it to, but it will probably be measured in months. If you've done lead generation campaigns before, take a look at them as examples and set your expectations accordingly.

PROVIDE MULTIPLE CONTACT CHANNELS

Not all prospects prefer to be contacted by phone. If you prospect only with phone calls, you won't connect with the prospects who would rather be contacted through social media or email. At the very least provide both a phone number and an email address in your lead generation tool. If you also include a social media page, a form on a website that prospects can fill out, and an additional phone number— the best option is your cell phone—you'll have even more success in collecting leads.

Make the Most of Every Lead

If you don't pursue every lead, you've wasted the time and money you invested in generating those leads. But often salespeople don't follow up all leads, feeling that some of them will not become sales. Of course, not all leads are equal, but you will never know for sure if a lead is valuable if you don't pursue it. Do at least a little basic research on each lead before you give up on it.

LEAD MANAGEMENT

Keep Them Organized

Odds are that on any given day you have a long list of leads to go through. A lead should stay on your radar until you have either closed the sale or shifted it to the "dead" pile, but the only way to keep an eye on every lead you get is to create a system that works for you.

CHOOSING A LEAD MANAGEMENT SYSTEM

There is no one best way to manage leads. Different salespeople have different approaches to the sales process. The best lead management system for you is the one that you can easily master and use intuitively. Here is a sampling of different lead management systems you might consider.

Customer Relationship Management (CRM) Software

This comes in dozens of different forms and can cost thousands of dollars—although many systems are quite cheap or even free. CRM programs are designed for lead management and usually come with report functions that make it easy to evaluate your successes and failures. Many CRM programs are cloud-based, meaning that they can be accessed remotely using a smartphone or other device.

Spreadsheets

These are fairly good for organizing lead information but aren't as flexible as CRMs. Maintaining a spreadsheet is as simple as entering new leads as you get them and removing old ones as they fizzle out. Spreadsheets generally don't have a way to generate reports about your leads, so tracking your progress isn't as easy as with a CRM.

Rolodexes

These are good ways to store leads on paper—for example, you can staple any business cards you receive right onto a Rolodex card. However, finding a particular lead in the Rolodex can be quite a challenge: you're limited to however much information you can squeeze onto the card, and worst of all, your entire lead list can be wiped out by a careless coffee spill. Few salespeople use a Rolodex as a primary lead management system these days.

Should You Keep Business Cards?

Salespeople who attend trade shows and other events typically collect fistfuls of business cards. If you use a paper-based lead management system, such as a Rolodex, by all means keep those cards. If not, feel free to enter the information into your computer system and toss the cards.

ORGANIZING YOUR LEADS

The leads you get probably come from lots of different sources, so you'll need to check for duplicates to keep from calling the same lead multiple times. Whenever you get new leads, enter them into a database or list. There are numerous tools that can simplify this task, such as image-to-text conversion programs.

Another way to ensure that your records are accurate is to write down every activity as soon as you complete it. If you don't enter your notes immediately, you'll be more likely to make an error or forget something important. Make a habit of entering your notes after making each call or sending each email.

Track each contact you have with a lead. Also note noncontact activities, such as researching a lead on a particular website, speaking with someone who isn't a decision-maker, or adding information to your lead's social media account. Keeping track of such minor details may seem like a bit much, but it will save time in the long run. For example, if you're Googling a potential client and check the first three sites you find, you want to enter the names of those sites so that you won't check them again when you do more research on that lead.

It's also wise to set up a regular schedule. That is to say, you might spend the first half hour of each day entering new leads, then the next hour researching those leads. After a fifteen-minute break, you could spend the remainder of the morning cold calling. Having a set routine can help you remain disciplined about doing the activities that you enjoy less, like cold calling, instead of skipping them.

You should also mark on your calendar any follow-ups you decide are necessary as soon as you finish an activity. For example, if you make a call to a lead and find out that the decision-maker you need to reach is on vacation until next Monday, add an entry to your calendar to call that lead next Tuesday. That way, you can be sure that you're making the most out of every lead. There are lots of calendar software programs out there, from the perennially popular Microsoft Outlook to a great many free calendars with a variety of features.

It's wise to keep your lead data in a central location where everyone on the sales team can access it as needed. It's certainly unproductive and even embarrassing if several people from your company call the same lead. This will also prevent such information from being lost if a salesperson leaves the company or changes territories. CRMs are the most efficient way to share such data, but even a Rolodex can be shared with the rest of the sales staff, as long as you make sure to explain your filing system to your associates.

CHAPTER 3

MAKING APPOINTMENTS AND QUALIFYING LEADS

Those leads that you turned up via prospecting are a precious resource. It's important to treat each of them with respect if you're to make enough sales. First, you'll need to select the best channel for contacting those leads. Phone calls and email are the most popular options for contacting leads, and each approach has its own pros and cons. If you don't reach the decision-maker by phone right away, leaving a compelling message will help ensure that he'll respond promptly. Once you get ahold of the prospect, your task is to convince him to make an appointment with you so that you can make your pitch. You'll also want to take some steps to make sure prospects *keep* those appointments. Finally, you'll need to decide whether you should qualify prospects before or during your sales appointments—or both.

REACHING YOUR LEADS

From Appointment to Presentation

Now that your prospecting efforts have turned up a number of leads, your next task is to get in touch with those leads, confirm that they are in fact prospects, and make an appointment to give them a full sales presentation. Getting in touch with new leads is typically done through cold calling.

Cold Calling Without a Phone

Cold calling is reaching out to potential customers without prior contact. Much cold calling takes place on the phone, but sending unsolicited emails, letters, and social media messages, and even dropping by in person, can all qualify.

Prospects are rarely happy to get a cold phone call from a salesperson. To understand this attitude, think about how you felt the last time *you* were on the receiving end of such a call. First, the call probably interrupted you in the middle of doing something you consider important: doing your job, having dinner with your family, or watching a show you'd been waiting all week to see. Second, you probably started the call with a feeling of skepticism about what the salesperson had offer you.

These attitudes are almost universal among prospects. To make your cold calling effective, you'll need to find a way past that barrier of resistance.

First, start out by acknowledging that you have interrupted the other person. The most common way to do so is by saying, "Is this a good time for you to talk?" However, some salespeople report that they get a more positive response by saying something like, "Have I caught you at a bad time?" The difference is that in the second version you're assuming that the prospect is busy right now. It shows a bit more respect for how busy he is. Experiment and see which approach works best for you.

Second, keep the focus on the prospect rather than on yourself. That means avoiding "I" statements in favor of "you" statements. So instead of saying, "I'm calling you today because…" or "I wanted to talk to you about…" try something like, "Executives in your industry have told me that security is a major concern for them. Is this also the case for you?" or "Have you heard about the new government regulation that will require stringent compliance measures for your industry?"

Third, go easy on the claims about your product and your company. Someone who's never met you is not going to be inclined to believe you or take your words at face value. Once you start talking about your product, it's easy to shift the focus back away from the prospect and onto yourself. So keep your claims believable and centered on the prospect and his concerns. For example, instead of saying, "This widget will reduce manufacturing costs by fifteen percent," try saying something like, "Many of my customers have reported that this widget reduced their manufacturing costs by fifteen percent or more. Depending on your manufacturing setup, I may be able to do something similar for you."

Fourth, always remember that the goal of your call is *not* to sell something to the prospect. Your goal at this time is to open a conversation with the prospect that will become the first step in a long and mutually lucrative relationship. To that end, you will usually try to set an appointment with the prospect so that you can expand further on the little bits of information you've given him during the cold call.

Sometimes you'll run across a prospect who will immediately ask for a price. This is a no-win situation for you because if the number is too high to suit your prospect, he will immediately say no thanks and hang up; and if by chance the number you give him sounds acceptable, he will focus on that number to the exclusion of everything else you say. Instead, politely decline to talk about price at this time. You can say something like, "I need to know more about your specific situation before I can give you a meaningful quote." Then propose an appointment so that you can get that information from your prospect.

Making cold calls over the phone is one of the most stressful situations that salespeople face. It's not surprising that many salespeople will do just about anything to avoid making cold calls. A little cold calling anxiety is harmless, possibly even beneficial. Being a bit on edge as you make calls can keep you sharp and on your game. But if you're stressed to the point where you have to force yourself to pick up the phone, you need to do something about it.

THE CURE FOR COLD CALLING ANXIETY

The first step to resolving your cold calling anxiety is to recognize it for what it is—an overreaction to the possibility that your call might lead to an unpleasant experience. Learn to recognize the symptoms so that you can start to distance yourself from them. Psychologists often teach phobia sufferers to step back and distance themselves from their fears by imagining that they are watching themselves as a character in a movie. Try it the next time you start to feel that dread in the pit of your stomach, and you may be surprised by how much it helps you to detach yourself from those negative feelings.

Physical action is also a great way to break a negative chain of thought. Stand up and walk briskly around the office for a minute, do ten jumping jacks, or play a song you really like and sing along—anything that gets you moving and thinking about happier things.

Finally, you need to retrain yourself into thinking of cold calls as a positive experience. This is an emotional process rather than a logical one. After all, it's your out-of-control emotions that are causing the problem; logic and reasoning won't do much to change your emotional state. So every time you finish a cold call, reward yourself in some way. Pick a reward that will perk up your spirits without disrupting your day. For example, popping an M&M after every call is a great option, but going out to lunch after every call won't work. Other possible rewards include getting up to look out the window and enjoying the view for a moment, sending an instant message to a friend or loved one (so long as you don't get drawn into a long conversation), and even taking a sip of tea.

GETTING LEADS TO RETURN YOUR MESSAGES

Leave a Killer Voicemail

If you place a cold call and find yourself in your lead's voicemail system, don't give up and hang up the phone. Voicemail provides a golden opportunity to get your lead to call *you* instead of spending days trying to chase her down yourself. But if you want to have your calls returned, you'll need to leave messages that will motivate the leads to get in touch with you. The following scripts can increase your chances of hearing back from leads.

SCRIPTS FOR LEAVING MESSAGES FOR NEW LEADS

If you're calling a new lead and you get her voicemail, here are some possible messages you can leave that are more likely to get her to call you back. Remember that the *whole point* of these calls is to get the appointment.

Increasing Revenues

"Hi, [prospect name]. This is [your name] with [your company]. You and I haven't spoken yet, but I've been doing some research on your company and I think you're a great fit for [product]. I know exactly how to [increase your revenues from X dollars to X dollars, reduce your costs by X percent, etc.], and I know you'll be happy if we spend a few minutes discussing how I can help you.

"When you get this message, please call me back at [your phone number]. That number again is [your phone number], and ask for [your name]. I look forward to speaking with you, and I guarantee you'll be glad you returned this call."

Solving a Problem

"Hello, [prospect name]. This is [your name] with [your company]. I need to speak with you briefly about how you're handling your [issue related to your product], because I have something that can solve [common problem]. Our clients include [list a few companies the prospect will know], and I know this approach will work for you as well. Believe me, it's worth a five-minute phone call to find out how.

"When you get this message, please call me back at [your phone number]. That number again is [your phone number], and ask for [your name]. I look forward to speaking with you, and thanks in advance for returning my call."

Presenting Ideas

"Good [morning/afternoon], [prospect name]. This is [your name] with [your company]. I read in the news about [fact about prospect, such as opening a new office], and I wanted to provide you with some ideas that may help with [issue related to fact]. We work with a lot of companies in the area, and I think you'll find it useful if we talk.

"When you get this message, please call me back at [your phone number]. That number again is [your phone number], and ask for [your name]. I look forward to speaking with you and to working with you in the future."

SCRIPT TO USE BEFORE
A SALES APPOINTMENT

Now that you've got the appointment, you need to follow up and make sure it happens. Make it clear that you're available if there is a last-minute change of plans by the client.

Demonstrating a Product

"Hello, [prospect name]. This is [your name] with [your company]. I'm just calling you for the appointment we have today at [time] to demonstrate [product]. You may be on the phone or finishing up a meeting, but when you get this message, please do give me a call.

"You can call me on my direct line, which is [your phone number]. I'll stay off the phone for a few minutes so that you can reach me easily. Once again, my direct number is [your phone number], and I look forward to speaking with you soon."

SCRIPT TO USE WHEN A PROSPECT
SEEMS TO BE DODGING YOU

Sometimes prospects get cold feet and start avoiding you. Here are some messages to leave that politely push them for a definite time and place where you can meet and discuss the product.

Asking for a Callback

"Hi, [prospect name]. This is [your name] with [your company] again. I'm sorry we haven't been able to get back in touch; if you're like me, I'm sure you're juggling quite a few projects. Do me a favor, though, and when you get this message, just call me back and leave me a voicemail with what you've decided to do about [product/proposal]. If you're still interested in it, great, but even if you've decided not to move forward with it, that's fine as well. Either way, it will be helpful for me to know."

Leaving Messages with Gatekeepers

If you get a decision-maker's assistant on the phone and he offers to take a message for you, you can use a variation of these scripts. You can also take the opportunity to ask questions, like, "What's the best time to call to reach Ms. Executive?"

At times sending an email or leaving a voicemail message can feel like dropping a message in a bottle and throwing it into the ocean. You're making the effort, but no one ever seems to respond to your attempts. Even the most provocative messages seem to vanish into the ether.

First, recognize the fact that your prospects and customers may never have gotten your message. Email will routinely get blocked by spam filters or run into other problems. Busy professionals may simply delete your voicemail messages without ever listening to them, because they don't recognize your phone number on caller ID. If you don't get a reply to a message, assume that the prospect never got it and don't feel rejected.

If the prospect did get the message but simply didn't respond, acting as though she never got it is still a good idea. If the first thing you say when you finally connect with the prospect is "Did you get my message?" you'll be starting off the conversation on the wrong foot. You've now put the prospect on the defensive by all but accusing her of ignoring your message. Instead, just paraphrase whatever you said in the message once you get her in person.

Using multiple channels to deliver your messages can also help. Some prospects rarely check their email but are diligent about checking voicemail, and vice versa. If you use email, phone, and possibly social media as well to connect with a prospect, you can feel pretty confident that at least one of those messages will get through. When you do get in touch with the prospect for the first time, be sure to ask which contact methods she prefers—and you can then use that method on subsequent attempts.

Also, don't give up on a prospect too easily. Salespeople, especially new salespeople, are generally not as aggressive on follow-up as they should be. It's likely that a prospect who has not responded is very busy right now and intends to talk to you later. If you leave a message or two and then give up, he'll just forget about you. But if you're persistent, you'll either outlast whatever crisis he's dealing with, or you'll finally manage to connect with him in person.

Another way to maximize the effect of your messages is to make it extremely easy for a prospect to respond. That means it's critical for you to always check your own messages and respond promptly. Give your prospects at least two different ways to reach out to you—phone and email at a minimum. If you can, include other contact options, such as social media or instant messaging. If your main business phone is not a cell phone, include your cell phone number in your voicemail greeting. This is especially important if you spend a lot of time out of the office, as many salespeople do.

When a prospect does get in touch with you based on a message, try to figure out what inspired the response. What did you do right?

If you ask every prospect who responds what motivated them to do so, you might uncover a common factor that you can then include in your future messages. Focus on what you did right rather than on what you did wrong; those are the details you'll want to repeat in future messages.

SELLING THE APPOINTMENT

Make Your Prospects *Want* to Meet You

A common rookie salesperson mistake is trying to close a sale with a prospect in a single cold call. When you pick up the phone and start cold calling, or walk into a neighborhood and start knocking on doors, the goal almost always should be to get an appointment with the decision-maker. Once you're at the actual appointment, you can start pitching the product, but in your first contact the only thing you should be pitching is an appointment.

START WITH A GREAT OPENER

If you can create an opener that surprises or intrigues prospects, you can break through their anti-salesperson rejection filter and really get their attention. The opener should be brief, personalized, and thought-provoking. Strong openers often include a question—this gets your prospects thinking about the answer, which can intrigue them enough to want to hear more from you.

For example, let's say you're selling supplements to veterinarians. Your cold call opener might be something like, "Hello, my name is Fred Smith and I'm with XYZ Company. I've worked with five veterinarians in your area and have increased their revenues by an average of $16,432 per month. Would you be interested in seeing similar revenue growth in your own office?"

You'll find more examples of great openers and ideas for creating your own openers in Chapter 8.

STATE YOUR BENEFITS

Your opener will have provoked the prospect into actually listening to what you have to say, so now's the time to start talking benefits. Here's where your pre-call research can really come in handy, since it can help you identify the most compelling benefit for that prospect. For example, if the prospect recently mentioned on *Facebook* that she's trying to cut back on spending, you can talk about how your product will save her money.

Benefits

Benefits are what a customer gets from using a product or service. If you identify and use a prospect's favored benefits, your sales pitch will be far more compelling.

Another option is to find a way to turn the appointment itself into a benefit. For example, if you're selling insurance, you might offer to give prospects an "insurance review" in which you look over their current policy and point out ways they might improve it. By offering your expertise at no charge, you're giving prospects something of value—and positioning yourself perfectly to make a sale.

CLOSE THE APPOINTMENT

It's just as important to close your cold calls as it is to close your sales. That means asking for an appointment rather than waiting for a prospect to admit she's interested. One of the strongest ways to get appointments is to just assume she's interested and move right on to the details. For example, you might say, "I've got time on my calendar on Wednesday afternoon and Thursday morning to meet with you and give you more information. Which works best for you?"

If the prospect isn't convinced, this is when she'll push back with one or more objections. If you're cold calling over the phone, have a list of common objections and responses handy so that you can quickly resolve these objections. (See Chapter 5 for more on handling objections.)

More Tips for Setting Appointments

- **Start with good leads.** This may seem like common sense, but salespeople sometimes don't realize how much the quality of their leads affects cold calling success rates.
- **Have a script.** Trying to "just wing it" is a lot more stressful, and you're also more likely to be at a loss for words at exactly the wrong moment.
- **Block out time for cold calling.** If you dread cold calling, as many salespeople do, it's easy to avoid it in favor of just about anything else. But if you set a specific time each day to cold call and *only* cold call, you'll have an easier time sticking to it.
- **Respect the gatekeeper.** Remember that the gatekeeper controls access to the decision-maker, so if that person likes you, your job will be a lot easier.
- **Smile.** It may sound silly, but when you smile as you're talking on the phone, the other person can actually hear the difference. Try it yourself if you don't believe it.
- **Have a strong opener.** You have only a few seconds to get the prospect's attention—don't waste them.
- **Don't sell the product.** The cold call is for getting the prospect interested enough to make an appointment, during which you'll deliver your actual sales pitch.

- **Do what it takes to feel more confident.** Whether that means writing out the best possible responses to common objections, researching your product in minute detail, or holding on to a rabbit's foot, go for it.
- **Find the best times to call and use them.** For example, it's often easier to reach decision-makers before 8:30 a.m.
- **Always leave a voicemail.** Have a message written out and ready to go so that you'll be able to leave the most effective message possible.
- **Go for the leaders.** When you're calling businesses, try to reach someone high up in the organization. That will help you avoid wasting time with non-decision-makers.
- **Believe in what you're selling.** If you don't truly believe that your product is good, no one else will. Know your product's flaws, but also know its good qualities.
- **Make more calls.** The more cold calling you do, the more prospects you'll be able to load into your pipeline.
- **Ask for the appointment.** Even if a prospect is interested, he probably won't be the one to suggest taking the next step—that's up to you.
- **Be honest.** It's better to tell the truth and lose the lead than it is to lie and taint your reputation.
- **Call when no one else is calling.** If you make calls on holidays, weekends, and other times when salespeople are unlikely to call, you will have a wide-open field.
- **Use emotion.** Prospects are more likely to get interested as a result of emotion rather than logic and reasoning.
- **Have fun!** Treat cold calling as a game. Try out new approaches, give yourself a small reward for each success, or do whatever else it takes to squeeze some joy out of the process.

MAKING APPOINTMENTS VIA EMAIL

Maximize Response Rates

Cold calling via the phone is still the most common way to reach out to leads, but cold emailing has become increasingly popular (as well as increasingly effective). You probably won't be able to completely replace phone calls with email messages, but once you get the hang of generating appointments via email, you'll be able to cut way down on your dialing.

The first major hurdle to overcome is getting your lead to read the email in the first place. Writing a compelling subject line is crucial. When your email arrives in someone's inbox, the first thing he sees is the subject line—and if the subject screams "salesperson," he won't even bother to open it. He doesn't know you, so your email address won't mean anything to him; the only thing he has to judge you on at this point is the email subject.

Spam Filters

Nearly everyone has spam filters on their email accounts, and those filters look particularly closely at the subject line. Certain spammy phrases make it very likely that your email will be junked. Phrases like *free*, *call now*, and *save big money* will usually trigger a spam filter.

Don't give in to the temptation to write a deceptive subject line, like, "Re: yesterday's meeting." You'll get your email opened, all right, but as soon as he realizes he doesn't know you, you've lost any chance to sell to him. The same goes for the body of the email. For example, some salespeople imply in their email subject or body that they've already emailed or called the prospect. If you really did email him, forward your original email so that he can see what you're referring to. If you really called, include a synopsis of your conversation or voicemail message.

Once you've come up with a good subject line, the next step is to craft an opening phrase that will keep him reading. This phrase should be similar to the hook you use in phone cold calling. In fact, if you have a good cold calling script, you can modify it and use it for emails as well. Just don't use it in an email to someone you've already called using the same script!

The very best opening line would be one that you customize to fit the prospect. For example, let's say you read a news article about a new tough regulation that affects a particular industry. Your emails to leads in that industry might start with, "Have you worked out a compliance game plan for Regulation X?" Then you can continue with a description of how your product or service can help with that need.

Don't use graphics or fancy formatting in your email. Ideally, it should look like an email that you'd send to a colleague at your company. No, it's not as pretty, but it looks professional rather than like a piece of marketing collateral, which means prospects will be more willing to read it. Also remember that some email clients won't download images by default, so if you include a lot of pictures, those prospects will get an email full of holes.

Most prospecting emails should be no more than a paragraph long—say, four to five sentences. Remember, the point is to get the prospect interested enough to get in touch with you, *not* to sell to him.

Always prominently include your company name and (if you have one) your company logo. It's also a good idea to include a slogan or other tagline related to your company. This will reassure prospects that you're not a random scammer and that you work for a legitimate company.

If you have something of value for the prospect, such as a white paper or how-to article, include a link in your email. People have a natural instinct to reciprocate when someone does something nice for them. If you give a prospect something useful or valuable without being prompted, he'll be strongly inclined to at least schedule an appointment with you.

Social Media for Cold Calling?

Social media is not a good choice for trying to get appointments with prospects. Instead, use it to intrigue prospects into contacting *you*. It's also a superb way to build a healthy business network, as you'll learn in Chapter 9.

Email works best in combination with other contact methods. Phone calls are a particularly good complement to email because phone calls are real-time and immediate, while email is less personal. Many people prefer one over the other, so if you use both, you'll be able to reach a wider range of decision-makers.

When using email to complement your phone cold calling, there are a few things to keep in mind. First, remember that your emails, unlike phone conversations, are permanent. So check them over at least once before you click Send, looking for both spelling and content errors. If anything seems unclear or dubious, rephrase it.

Second, emails should generally be brief and to the point. If you have a long or complicated point to make, state in your email that the issue is too complex to cover in an email and you're going to give the prospect a call so that you can explain things over the phone.

Sending an email message and then following up with a voicemail makes it extremely easy for prospects to respond in one manner or the other. This works especially well if you link the two without giving precisely the same information. For example, you might leave a voicemail mentioning that you saw a report that will help this prospect with a certain problem you know he's been experiencing, and then follow up with an email that has a link to the report in it.

GETTING PROSPECTS TO KEEP APPOINTMENTS

How to Be Sure They'll Show Up

After you first speak with a prospect (which will usually happen as part of a cold call), send her a brief email that includes the date, time, and place you've agreed on for your sales appointment. Not only does this help cut down on "oops, I forgot about you" on the day of the meeting, but it also gives you an opportunity to include a link or two in your email that provides useful and interesting information. You might link to an article on a topic you discussed during the cold call, or a document that relates to the prospect's business. This helps you to get off on the right foot with her and also to begin building your reputation as a helpful, experienced contact.

Following Up versus Stalking

Sending one or two reminders is a good business practice, but sending ten is overkill. If your prospects are avoiding you to that extent, leave them alone for a while. You can always try to reach them a few weeks or months down the line.

Sending a reminder after you schedule the appointment, and perhaps a second reminder the day before the appointment, is usually sufficient. However, if you weren't as convincing as you thought you were during the cold call, it's possible that the prospect just agreed to what you were saying to get you off the phone. With a little effort, you can learn to spot these types of reluctant prospects and may even be able to turn them around.

NO REAL NEED

If a prospect thinks that your product's latest model is really cool-looking but the model he bought last year is working just fine, he probably won't be interested enough in your updated version to buy one right now. If the prospect really doesn't need what you're offering, you're unlikely to close a sale—at least, not yet.

Questions like, "Have you had a product similar to this one before?" and "Is the model you have now meeting your needs?" will help you identify your prospect's level of motivation. If you realize that your prospect isn't really interested at this time, ask other questions to determine when he *will* be more interested in buying a new product. One useful piece of information, for example, is when the warranty on the product he has now will expire. Then you can log this information and call him around the expiration date.

NOT A GOOD FIT

Sometimes your product just won't have the features that the prospect wants. If a prospect needs a widget that spins at 150 rpm and your best model reaches only 120 rpm, there's not much you can do about it. Of course, miscommunications do happen, so it's also possible that the prospect thinks your product isn't right for her when it actually does have all the features she needs.

Again, doing a little qualifying before the appointment can help. Ask which features are important to the prospect, and if your product doesn't have those features, let her know. If your product does have all of the features she wants, then be sure to bring up each of those features in your presentation and emphasize how well your product would meet all the prospect's needs and preferences.

NEVER INTENDED TO BUY

Some buyers like to periodically check on their current supplier's competitors, just to make sure that they're getting a good deal. They will set up appointments with salespeople and may even attend those appointments without ever intending to buy anything. Particularly savvy and price-conscious buyers will sometimes even run through the entire sales process with you just to squeeze a better deal out of your competitor ("You see, Mr. Salesperson, Jane Smith from ABC Widgets is offering me a ten percent discount. What can you do for me?").

Unfortunately, these tricky folks can be hard to spot because it's a game they're usually very good at playing. If you suspect that you've been sucked into this kind of situation, you can always ask the buyer flat-out if that's the case. By then, the sale is dead anyway, so you've nothing to lose—and you might impress the prospect with your savvy, potentially opening the door for future sales with him.

RISK-AVERSE

To be successful in sales, it is vital to build trust between you and your prospects. If you don't create good relationships with them, they may very well be unable or unwilling to move beyond their natural concerns about making a mistake. If you actually succeed in reaching them, they'll very likely say that they need to "think about it" and then will somehow always manage to be out of the office when you call them back.

This happens for a couple of reasons. It may be that you haven't spent enough time showing the prospect that you are trustworthy. It's also possible that you haven't addressed all of their objections. To deal with this situation, you must find out and address the prospect's most pressing concern and explain how your product can solve it. Remember that fear is the reason the prospect is holding back, so pressuring him will only exacerbate the situation.

CRUCIAL QUALIFYING QUESTIONS

Uncovering the Most Important Details

Qualifying your leads helps you to separate the wheat (actual prospects) from the chaff (people who can't or won't buy from you no matter what). Qualifying usually takes the form of asking a few stock questions that are designed to identify the factors that all prospects share. For example, you wouldn't have much luck selling auto insurance to someone who doesn't have a car, so the question "Do you own or lease a vehicle?" would be a good qualifying question for that product. Once you've sorted out your leads and identified the true prospects, you can keep moving through the sales process with those prospects.

How thoroughly you qualify prospects is up to you. Typically, if you're selling a very expensive product or service, you'll have a few, very large sales during each quota cycle. In that case it makes sense to qualify thoroughly so that you don't spend a great deal of time with someone who was never going to buy from you. On the other hand, if you make tons of small sales, you'll probably do just a minimum of qualifying. As you become more familiar with the products and customers, you'll become adept at identifying the most important qualifying questions and won't need to ask so many.

Salespeople also need to decide just when they will do their qualifying. There are two main times to qualify prospects: during the cold call, and during the appointment. It's usually wise to ask at least a few qualifying questions during the cold call so that you can weed out the obvious non-prospects. If your qualifying process is usually brief, you might just want to get the entire thing over with during the call. However, if you have an in-depth qualifying process, you'll likely want to save the bulk of your questions for the appointment itself. By that point, your prospect has already shown a certain level of interest and will be more willing to cooperate with a lengthy question and answer session.

Custom Qualifying

If you look at the data on your best customers, you'll probably see some similarities. Asking questions that identify those factors is a great way to spot the most valuable prospects. You can then prioritize those prospects and watch your sales numbers soar!

Whether you commence qualifying during cold calls or at appointments, these sample questions will help you figure out what to ask your prospects.

- Have you purchased a product/service like this before? How did it work out?
- (If they already own a competitor's product) What do you like and dislike about your current product?
- (For B2B sales) What's your purchasing process for products like this?
- What's your deadline for purchasing this product or one like it?
- Are you the sole decision-maker?
- (If they say no to the previous question) May I contact the other decision-maker(s) and invite them to join us?
- What's your budget for this purchase?

- How much have you spent in the past on similar purchases?
- What features are most important to you in this product/service?
- How much help would you like with installation/training/implementation? (Pick the one that best matches what your company offers.)
- What are the most important challenges or problems you're dealing with right now?
- What problems do you hope to solve by using this product/service?
- What motivated you to consider this purchase?
- (If they respond to the previous question with something like, "Hey, *you* called *me*!") Why haven't you been considering a purchase until now?

As you practice qualifying prospects, you'll learn which questions are most helpful in identifying non-prospects. Those are the questions to prioritize, so that you can eliminate non-prospects as early as possible and keep from wasting your time and theirs.

CHAPTER 4

SALES PITCHES AND PRESENTATIONS

The sales presentation is your chance to shine. You've got thirty minutes or so to uncover the prospect's needs and show how your product will address those needs. Depending on what you're selling, you may need several appointments before the prospect is ready to buy. This is particularly true for B2B salespeople, as companies often have complex buying processes with many decision-makers. But if you mess up your presentation, you won't be getting any future meetings—or sales—from that prospect. Prior preparation and research are crucial to delivering an effective presentation. You'll need to use product benefits to show prospects what they're missing and prove value. If you're presenting to remote prospects, you'll need to master the art of virtual sales presentations. It's a lot to learn, but by the time you finish reading this chapter, you'll have a basic understanding of all these matters.

BASIC PRESENTATION TIPS

How to Be a Better Speaker

Communication skills are extremely important for salespeople, and that includes the ability to make a good presentation. Your sales presentation is your big chance to get prospects excited about buying your product or service. A few things to keep in mind while making any presentation include:

- As a rule of thumb, plan for your presentation to last no more than sixty minutes. Tell your audience approximately how long you'll be talking, and stick to it.
- Stand up while you speak. Sitting puts pressure on your diaphragm, which makes your voice softer and lowers your energy level.
- If someone mentions that she's had a particular problem, stress how your product can help solve her problem. If your audience is kind enough to tell you their hot buttons, don't waste it!
- If your audience is nodding at what you have to say or leaning forward in their seats, they like what they're hearing. If they're leaning back with arms crossed, they're skeptical. Snoring is also a bad sign.
- Give specific, real-life examples. Find an example of someone who did exactly what you're proposing with your product or service, and tell their story. If you can't find an exact example, at least bring testimonials from satisfied customers.

Many salespeople find themselves giving sales presentations to large groups of people, especially in complex B2B sales. You might have to present to multiple decision-makers, end users, lawyers, purchasing agents, department heads, etc., all at the same time. Speaking to a large group of people is very different from speaking to just one or two—and it's often unnerving for the speaker.

Practice, Practice, Practice

If you're new to sales and don't have public speaking experience, take every opportunity to practice speaking in front of a group. Offer seminars, volunteer to teach a class, or join a group like Toastmasters. The more you practice, the more comfortable you'll be in an actual sales presentation.

When you're addressing just one person, your presentation can be more of a conversation, and you may not need to structure it in advance (although you should still have your main talking points either memorized or on a note in front of you). That isn't an option when you are speaking to several people at a time. As you'll probably be more nervous in front of a bigger audience, your mind is more likely to go blank at the wrong moment. Advance preparation will give you more confidence when you speak, and having a script ready will give you something to fall back on if your ingenuity fails you.

It is important that the pace of your presentation be slow. Even if you think you're speaking at the right speed, it's common to be going too fast for the audience, and if you're nervous, that's even more likely. To get a better perspective on how your presentation sounds, practice it once with an audio recorder or in front of someone else.

Be especially careful to enunciate your words clearly—a large audience is unlikely to interrupt your presentation to let you know that they don't understand what you're saying. Use short, simple words as much as possible; they are more effective in selling and are also easier to hear.

If possible, stand where you can glance inconspicuously at a clock to avoid speaking too long because you've lost track of time. If you're almost out of time and you have more information to cover than the time allows, you can either jump to the end of your presentation or ask the audience if it would be all right to take some extra time. Never assume that they don't mind running an extra half hour; let them know that you respect their time by asking for permission.

Every so often pause your presentation and ask a question of the audience, either a question related to the presentation (for example, "Is this an issue you've dealt with in the past year?") or a status question (such as "Does that make sense?"). Breaking the flow of your presentation with some interaction helps to keep your audience interested—and alert! If you see people glancing at their watches and/or eyes starting to glaze over, throw in a question or two to bring their attention back to what you're saying.

VISUAL AIDS

When using visual aids (for example, presentation software slides), keep them simple. Slides should enhance what you're saying, not distract the audience from your words. Don't read the text on each slide. If it's too small for the audience to see clearly, you should modify the slide. People can read faster than you can speak, so reciting from something they can see for themselves will just annoy them.

Finally, always be early when you give big presentations to allow a generous amount of time to check out the space and make sure that you have everything you need. The more complex your presentation is, the more important it is to do this. If you need your host to provide certain items, such as a projector, a heavy table for your demonstration model, or even just some pens and slips of paper to pass out, arrive especially early. That way, if it turns out that the promised supplies are not available, you'll have a chance to either change your plans or rush out and get the missing items.

WRITING A PITCH THAT SELLS

For a great sales presentation you need a great script. Coming up with your pitch on the fly just won't work well—you'll end up repeating yourself, inadvertently leaving out crucial information, not having good comebacks for common objections, and so on. Your script doesn't have to dictate every word you say, but it should at least create the framework for your presentation. Draft it well in advance and then rehearse it until you have it thoroughly memorized. Here are some guidelines:

- The opening sentence or two of a sales presentation may determine whether your prospects listen raptly or tune you out. If you have a great point to make or a strong hook, put it in as your very first line.
- Your script doesn't have to be just words. You can include stage directions to remind yourself when to pause, when to make eye contact, and so on. Keep the tone conversational—you don't want to sound like the audio version of a sales brochure.
- Anything you write for sales purposes needs to evoke an emotional response in your listener (or reader). Interestingly, negative emotions are more likely to hook prospects than positive

ones—most people will respond more strongly to the fear of losing something than they will to the hope of gaining something. Experts say that the biggest motivators are fear, greed, guilt, exclusivity, anger, salvation, and flattery.

- Presentation software can be a fantastic way to convey information or a fast way to put participants to sleep in their chairs. If you choose to create a slide deck, make sure that you use it as a visual stimulus rather than a teleprompter. Prioritize slides full of images, photos, and diagrams, and include just enough text to clarify those images. Keep each slide as simple and uncluttered as possible. And if you can, grab a photo related to the prospect— a shot of their office building or home, perhaps—and add it to the slide deck.

An Alternative

Presentation software isn't the only way to add a visual element to your presentation. If the room has a whiteboard, you can use it to enhance your presentation with simple diagrams and sketches. *Whiteboard Selling*, by Corey Sommers and David Jenkins, gives an excellent overview of the concept.

- Features tell, benefits sell, and nowhere is that truer than in a sales presentation. Benefits give prospects a reason to want to buy the product. They also tend to call up an emotional response, whereas features speak to the logical part of the mind. And buying decisions nearly always stem from emotions.
- Keep track of news reports related to your industry and/or your main customers' industry. If you see something interesting and timely, like a new discovery or a regulation that's just been

passed, work it into your presentation. This gives you credibility as an expert and adds urgency to your call to action.

- Work a story or two into your presentation. Stories interest people, and stories about someone like them help listeners imagine themselves in that person's place. Do let prospects know that your story is fictional, not a testimonial (unless it really did happen). For added impact you can come up with a generic story and then customize it to fit specific prospects. For example, if you know a prospect is very interested in saving time, then make the story about how your product did just that for a particular imaginary person.

- Show your prospect that the product you're selling is actually worth much more than its price tag. One way to manage this is by citing examples of customers who have saved money or averted expensive disasters by using your product—the more specific the example, the better. If you can use actual numbers (e.g., "Company X saved $11,433 during the first quarter on copying costs alone"), that's best of all.

- The more you know about your prospects, the better you can tune your writing to pique their interests. If you are presenting to a single decision-maker, do some quick research on the prospect and use that information in your pitch. For example, if you see from the customer's *LinkedIn* page that he is going on a business trip to China next month, you could work that into your presentation (e.g., "Our next-day delivery option will get the product out to you weeks before you leave the country, so you'll have plenty of time to set it up first.").

- Ask your existing customers for testimonials and work one or two into your script. Testimonials lend your presentation what psychologists call "social proof." The fact that your prospect's peers approve of your product gives you a big boost of credibility, while peer pressure will help nudge the prospect closer to a buying decision.

- After you've finished writing your presentation script, read it out loud while you record yourself and then play back the recording. Does it flow, or does it sound stilted and overly formal? Listening to your own presentation is a great way to see if it's hitting the mark in tone and will help you to spot any errors. Better yet, record a video and check your body language as well as your tone.

BENEFITS VERSUS FEATURES

Sell the Sizzle, Not the Steak

Practically all basic sales training emphasizes the need to present benefits rather than features to prospects during your pitch, because doing so will make an enormous difference in your success as a salesperson. "Features" are the product's basic attributes, while "benefits" are what the customer will get from those features. For example, a frying pan's list of features might include a nonstick finish. A benefit of that feature is convenience: customers can put food directly in the pan without needing to grease it first.

How to Tell Benefits from Features

If you're not sure if something is a benefit or a feature, ask yourself, "Is this something I'd get out of using the product?" A nonstick finish isn't something you get out of a frying pan, but less prep time and less cleaning time are.

Try this exercise: make a list of every feature for one of the products or services you sell, and then make a second list of all the benefits you can think of that are associated with each of those features. If you really work at it, you can probably come up with several times as many benefits as features. Take that frying pan again: if you don't think the convenience benefit would be convincing to a particular prospect, you could instead talk about how the customer might find it easier to lose weight using this pan because he won't be using as much oil and will reduce his calorie intake. Or you could talk about how easy it will be to clean the pan, because food doesn't get stuck on and have to be soaked or scraped off. All of these benefits relate back to the single feature of being nonstick.

Once you get comfortable talking about benefits, you can take your presentation a step further and focus on solutions. Benefits are compelling because they give prospects a reason to want to buy. When you pair those benefits with a prospect's most compelling needs, you are able to present solutions: a direct link between what the product does and how it will solve the prospect's problems.

Think about it this way. When someone goes to the hardware store and buys a drill, it's not because he wants to have a drill—it's because he wants to have a hole in the wall. The products and services that we sell are just a means to an end.

Prospects will talk to you only if they have either an issue or an opportunity in some way related to your product. If a prospect has no need, he won't bother to take the time to listen to your sales presentation. The trick is to identify that desired outcome and then build your sales presentation around it.

Start by looking at your sales presentation to see how much you are focusing on the idea of owning the product and how it will enhance the prospect's life. Using a story to present this idea is a particularly powerful way to shift the prospect's mindset. As much as a third of your presentation should be about ownership of the product and how the prospect will feel when his problem is solved or his opportunity realized.

Of course, in order to frame your presentation around solutions, you'll need to know what the solutions are. The first place to look for this information is your current customer base. Speak with several different customers and find out how they use your product and what they get out of it. This will probably give you several different ideas that you can work into your presentation.

But tossing potential solutions at your prospects won't do you much good. If you list ten benefits and your prospect is interested in only one or two of them, he's going to be pretty unimpressed. Instead, when you meet with a prospect, ask questions to uncover the specific solution that he is looking for.

Asking questions during your presentation is a good idea for a lot of reasons. It gets the prospect involved in a conversation, instead of leaving him in the position of a passive audience member. It helps build rapport by showing him that you're interested in what he needs and not just in making a quick sale. And, of course, it gives you the information you need to laser-focus your sales presentation on the subjects that will interest him the most.

If you've done a good job polling your existing customers, then the needs that you uncover during questioning will usually be a pretty close match to some of the needs your existing customers cited. This makes it easy to come up with a list of solutions for those needs ahead of time, so you don't have to make up something on the spot. Inevitably, no matter how thorough you are, you'll occasionally meet someone with a brand-new problem or opportunity. In that case you'll need to think on your feet, but at least you'll be able to add another solution to your list for future presentations.

When you're asking questions, pay attention to the prospect's body language and tone of voice. The more emotion he shows, whether positive or negative, the more important that issue is to him. If he's very emotional about a particular subject, it means that he feels more urgency about resolving it. Those are the "hot button" issues that you can emphasize in your presentation. The more you focus in on the needs and solutions that matter most to a prospect, the more likely you will be to close the sale.

PREPPING FOR PRESENTATIONS

Ready, Set...

You've made an appointment with a prospect, and you've got your script written and memorized. Before you head into the presentation, you've got a little more work to do if you want to maximize your odds of making a sale.

Putting together a plan for every appointment may seem like a bother, but it's worth the effort. If you've done the necessary research in advance, you can avoid follow-up calls and meetings. Doing pre-appointment planning generally shortens your sales cycle, meaning that you can proceed to the next prospect (and the next sale) much more quickly.

The first step in developing your plan is to figure out what it is you want to accomplish. Sometimes your goal is to close the sale, but in more complicated sales situations it will often require several meetings to get to closing. For example, your goal in the first appointment might be getting the decision-maker to agree to a longer appointment so that you can make your full pitch.

The next step will be to consider what issues might keep you from reaching the goal you set in the first step. Work up a list of the problems that you might encounter, especially if you often see them at this point in your sales process. For example, in the scenario depicted earlier one problem you might encounter in getting decision-maker approval could be correctly identifying the decision-maker, so that you pitch to the right person.

Third, determine what you'll need to find out from the prospect in order to proceed. In the early stages of the sales cycle this will include getting the information necessary to qualify the prospect.

Once you've accomplished that, you'll need more detailed information from your prospect so that you can be sure your pitch is personalized for her.

Fourth, try to determine what questions the prospect is likely to ask you and prepare some good answers. Some of the questions may be about product features and similar topics, but others will likely be objections. Whenever you hear a new question when you're on an appointment, take the time after the appointment to write down a good answer. That way, if you encounter that question again, you'll have the answer ready.

Fifth, and possibly most important, you need to determine what value you'll provide to the prospect in return for taking the time to meet with you. The value you provide could be an object, like a freemium (a low-value product or service provided for free) or white paper, or it could be just a useful piece of information that you share with her. Whatever it is, it should be something that the prospect will appreciate. If the prospect doesn't see what you offer as something useful to her, the most valuable item in the world will be worthless.

Do I Really Need to Do Research?

Not all salespeople need to do major pre-presentation research. The more expensive the item you sell, the more research you'll likely need to do. More expensive items typically mean fewer sales per year, so every sale will matter. That makes the time spent on research well worth your while.

Doing research is a crucial part of preparing for any sales presentation. The more information you have ahead of time, the easier it will be for you to pitch the prospect. Such research can give you valuable clues as to the prospect's goals or pain points. For example, a prospect who complains on *Facebook* about how bad customer service has gotten these days will likely respond to a pitch emphasizing your company's fabulous service.

The best sources to use for your research will vary depending on what you're selling, what industry you're selling to, and whether you are selling to consumers or other businesses. However, there are some sources that are pretty universally useful. *Google* is probably the best-known research source. Enter the prospect's name, and you're likely to get a plethora of results. Most search engines will provide equivalent results, so use whichever one you're most comfortable with.

The prospect's own website is almost a mandatory stop for research. Nearly every business and a huge number of individuals have their own websites, often providing a wealth of information about them. It's also a good idea to check the various social media sites and browse through whatever accounts your prospect might have. Since these particular research sources are actually written by the prospect herself, they can give you insight into how she thinks and what's most important to her.

The Internet isn't your only source of useful data. Industry events, directories, and reference books are all great places to learn more about a specific business or type of business. Newspapers and magazines can give insight into the current state of the business or industry in question. For example, you might learn about pending legislation that will have a major impact on the prospect or find out about a recent recall of their products.

When doing research, keep in mind that there's a lot of bogus information floating around, especially on the Internet. Basing a sales presentation on bad information is even worse than not doing any research at all. The rule of thumb is to only use information that you found in at least two different places, preferably very different places—for example, on an industry website and in a *New York Times* article. Many sites will take information directly from other sites without verifying it first, so if you find something repeated on another site using exactly the same wording, it doesn't count as a second source.

The most certain way to verify information is to ask the prospect herself. However, that may not be an option, especially if you want to know *before* the sales presentation. In that case a better option might be to ask a contact in the same industry or a subject matter expert. If you can't find verification, don't use that bit of information in your presentation no matter how temptingly juicy it might seem.

COMMON PRESENTATION ERRORS

Don't Make These Mistakes

If you're not getting the results you'd like from your sales presentations, you may be making one or more of these common mistakes.

RESPONDING TO OBJECTIONS BEFORE THEY ARISE

When the same objection comes up repeatedly in sales presentations, it's easy to assume that every prospect is thinking about that particular issue. But it's a mistake to bring up *any* issue before the prospect does. If you raise an issue that the prospect hadn't thought of yet, you can be sure he'll be thinking about it now.

Getting Prospects to Present

You may be wondering how you can listen more than you speak when you're the one giving the presentation. The answer is to ask the kinds of questions that get a prospect talking at length. Once you learn the right questions, you'll find that prospects often talk *themselves* into buying.

TALKING MORE THAN LISTENING

Extreme extroverts are less likely to become great salespeople than moderate extroverts or introverts, despite the stereotypes. That's because in sales listening is at least as important as talking. Remember, you have one mouth and two ears, and you should honor that fact by listening twice as much as you talk.

PROMISING TOO MUCH

Sometimes it's hard to resist the urge to overpromise. For example, if you're short of meeting your quota and time is running out, doing a little overpromising to secure a sale seems like the easy way out. Or if the prospect is already mad at you because you've made a mistake, it's tempting to promise whatever it takes to make them happy with you. But if you make a promise and then don't follow through, you've lost that prospect's trust, probably forever. Building trust is hard enough when you're not sabotaging yourself, so when you make a promise, be absolutely sure that you can keep it.

Discounting

Many salespeople see discounts as the easy way to secure a sale, and sometimes a nice discount does indeed enable you to seal the deal. However, there's a hidden cost to a heavy discounting habit. First, it teaches your customer that the sticker price on your products isn't the "real" price. That means that every time the customer in question buys from you, he'll expect an additional discount. Second, those discounts you're offering come directly out of your company's profit margin. If discounting gets widespread enough, you can literally put your company out of business by killing off its profit. If you're struggling to close a sale, try other methods before resorting to offering a price discount. Or better yet, just say no to discounting altogether. (Discounting will be discussed further in Chapter 5.)

NOT DISCOVERING THE PROSPECT'S NEEDS

Prospects aren't interested in products; they're interested in outcomes. No prospect wants a bigger (and more expensive) battery on his cell phone; he wants to be able to talk on the phone for hours without running out of juice. Or he wants to be able to carry the phone around for several days without charging it. Or he wants to know that in a power outage, even if his phone isn't at full charge, he'll still be able to make calls. But you won't know which outcome the prospect desires unless you ask the right questions. Uncovering the prospect's needs before you start making a pitch allows you to aim your pitch in the right direction to get the prospect's interest. Without that information there's a good chance that your sales pitch, no matter how compelling, will miss the mark.

SELLING TO NON-DECISION-MAKERS

Not everyone in a company (or a family, for that matter) is authorized to make decisions. The trouble is that non-decision-makers might not clue you in right away. So if you start selling to the first person who answers the phone, you might actually get through multiple phone calls and/or meetings before realizing that the person you've been working with is not authorized to buy from you. That's a huge amount of wasted time and energy that you could have been spending moving a sale forward. Before you put a lot of energy into someone you think is a prospect, verify that she's the decision-maker. It's also a good idea to check if there will be multiple decision-makers involved in the purchase, so that you can hopefully talk to them all at once. If you identify all the decision-makers from the beginning, you also won't get a nasty surprise when you think you're about to close a sale but instead find out that you've been pitching to the wrong person.

NOT FOLLOWING UP

Some prospects seem unable to make a decision. Others have to follow complex and extended buying processes that make everything take a long time. For prospects like these, how and when you follow up is critical. Generally, any meeting that doesn't end with a sale ought to end with setting a date and time for a follow-up with the prospect. Then make sure you contact him on schedule. If you don't claim ownership of the task of following up, you can be certain your prospect won't be the one to do it.

VIRTUAL PRESENTATIONS

Presenting Globally

When you've got prospects all over the country, you can't exactly give a lot of on-site sales presentations. Fortunately, modern technology makes it relatively easy to hold virtual meetings that are almost as effective as in-person ones.

You don't want to log in to a meeting only to discover that your webcam isn't working. Check all your equipment ahead of time and confirm that it's all functioning.

Being punctual is basic courtesy. Let the other attendees know how long you'll take, and then stick to that time line religiously. That means budgeting time in your presentation for questions and clarifications. If the meeting starts to go off on a major tangent, ask the others if you can discuss that point later and then return to your planned presentation.

Video or Webinar?

Video is usually the best option for giving sales presentations. Webinars are more appropriate for training and demos. However, if all you have on hand is webinar software, it's certainly better than nothing.

There are two main kinds of virtual sales presentations. The first is the webcam or video presentation, in which you and the prospect communicate by using video conferencing, sitting in front of webcams. The second is a webinar presentation, in which a slideshow on your computer monitor appears on the client's monitor and you take him through the slides. When you do webinar presentations, you will generally be on the phone with the prospect while you review the slides. Alternatively, some webinar software will let you communicate using the computer's microphone and speakers.

Webcam presentations are very much like on-site presentations because you and the prospect can see one another. However, the prospect can see only the finite area shown by the webcam, so that is where his attention will be focused. It's important to stage the area behind you before you make the call. Move anything that might distract the prospect out of his line of sight, or attach a Webaround screen to the back of your chair to block his vision of what's behind you.

Place your webcam and monitor so that you're not backlit by a bright window; otherwise, the prospect will only be able to see your silhouette. It's also important to be sure that your webcam is positioned so that the other participants can see your entire face.

You definitely don't want anyone to walk in during your presentation and interrupt it by asking what you want for lunch or something similarly disruptive. If you can, put your computer in an unused office with a door, and close the door. In fact, if your colleagues have a habit of walking in without knocking, lock the door!

If there is no unused space available, put up a sign that says, "MEETING IN PROGRESS," and make sure your coworkers know they must not interrupt you unless the building is on fire. Turn off your landline and cell phone ringers and possibly even your email client and chat software until the call is completed, so that you won't be distracted by the chime of incoming messages.

The disadvantage of doing a webinar presentation is that you can't see your prospect, which means you won't be able to read his body language. The solution is to make your presentation very interactive. Every few slides, ask a question or invite a comment. That way, you will keep the prospect interested, and his tone of voice will give you an indication of how he's feeling.

The rules for selecting the slides you use for your webinar should be similar to those governing the choice of slides—keep each slide simple and brief, don't inundate the prospect with complex graphs and charts, and include enough images to keep your listener from drowning in text.

Start the webinar with something that will capture the prospect's attention and give him a hint about what benefits might be in store for him. For example, you might start the webinar by bringing up the prospect's main concern, which you discovered through your research or during the cold call, and then present a brief example of how you helped another customer solve the same problem.

Even if you have a good headset, it's harder for people to follow you in a virtual meeting than in a face-to-face one. You should make an effort to talk more slowly and to speak as clearly as possible. Speaking slowly and clearly not only makes it much easier for others to understand you, but it also tends to catch their attention and makes it less likely that the other attendees will tune you out. If you're speaking carefully, it's also less likely that you'll say the wrong thing!

In order to use either video or webinar sales presentations, you'll need to get the right software package. There are plenty of video conferencing and webinar services to choose from, ranging in price from free to hideously expensive. Not surprisingly, the free and low-priced packages have little technical support and are often lacking in features, while top-end providers may have features you'll never need. It's best to start with a free or very cheap provider and try it for a presentation or two. You can always upgrade to a more expensive version if you don't like it.

HOW TO PROVE VALUE

What They'll Get for Their Money

The popularity of consultative selling has resulted in the development of value-added selling as a sales approach. In value-added selling the salesperson presents the service or product but then adds something special to add to the value of the product. Value-added selling not only helps make your product stand out from the competition; it also gives your prospects a reason to purchase the product from you instead of buying it on the Internet.

Consultative Selling

Consultative selling means that the salesperson positions himself as a problem-solver and works with prospects to find solutions for their needs. It's sometimes called solution-based selling because of its focus on finding solutions.

The type of value you add will vary depending on the type of product you sell. A value item must be both unique (or at least unusual) and of worth to the customer in order to help motivate her to buy. Some value items will be seen as highly useful to buyers in one marketplace but will seem worthless to the buyers in another.

If a prospect is willing to talk to you at all, it's because she knows that she needs to make a change. It's usually not difficult to uncover the needs that have led the prospect to consider a purchase; in fact, many prospects will come right out and tell you if you give them a chance. If you can repeat back the prospect's needs to her and then clearly state how your product will resolve those needs, you've just established a pretty strong value for your product.

By the time they arrive at a sales presentation all prospects are aware that they may have a problem, but many are not aware of other problems they're facing or how serious those problems are. If you can uncover these problems for the prospect, you'll move yourself a whole lot closer to closing the sale. If you can also show how your product will resolve those problems, you've got an excellent chance of sealing the deal.

Showing how your product is different (and better) than a competitor's product is one of the major components of adding value. You've got to find some way to stand out from the pack in order to conclusively show your prospect why she should be buying from you instead of from someone else.

If you decide to differentiate your product by pointing out that it's the only one that comes in glitter colors, you're not going to have a lot of success. When adding value, you must pick something that matters to a prospect. Ideally, choose factors that are both important to your prospect and that she needs to resolve or address quickly.

Saying that your product is better than that of Company X is a start, but it's probably not enough to really motivate a prospect. After all, the prospect barely knows you at this point and has little reason to trust you. The more proof you can bring to the table, the better. Testimonials are a great place to start, especially if you can come up with one that represents a customer who's very similar to your prospect. Other good sources of proof are articles, reports, studies, and other third-party write-ups.

WHAT PROSPECTS HAVE IN COMMON

Every prospect is a little different, but most will share a few common needs and priorities. A way of adding value that will apply to a wide range of prospects is much stronger than one that will interest only a few. If you have a half dozen such ideas written up and ready to present, you will be able to pique the interest of almost any prospect you might meet. That puts you in a much stronger position than if you had to come up with a new one on the fly for each new prospect.

These days everybody has too much to do and not enough time to do it in. Your prospects are not immune to this problem any more than you are. While a prospect might otherwise be interested in what you have to say, he will hesitate to set an appointment with you simply because there are ten other things that he should be doing with that time.

The answer to this dilemma is to give prospects something in return for the time they're giving you by *adding value to the sales appointment itself*. Not only does this motivate prospects to meet with you in the first place, but they will also be grateful to you for respecting the fact that they took the time to meet with you.

The first and cardinal rule of adding value to sales appointments is never wasting the prospect's time. During the cold call ask at least a few basic qualifying questions to confirm that the person you're speaking with is actually a prospect. You probably won't be able to completely qualify during the cold call, but you can at least rule out the most obvious non-prospects.

If you can add enough value to the meeting that your prospects feel that they've actually gained something important from showing up, you'll find it much easier to get future appointments with them (and anyone they might refer to you). For example, if your research uncovers an issue that your prospect is facing, you might want to track down an article or white paper that addresses that issue and bring it with you to the meeting. Even if the information you bring is something the prospect already knew, you've shown that you care about helping him—so at a minimum you'll have built some rapport with your prospect.

CHAPTER 5
HANDLING OBJECTIONS

In sales terminology an objection is a concern that the prospect has about buying your product. Your prospect might choose to describe that concern in detail ("What if it breaks down?") or just give you a vague delaying statement ("I'll think about it."). You may run across objections at various points in the sales cycle, but the most crucial time for handling objections is right before you close. If you haven't dealt with them successfully by that point, the sale will come to a screeching halt. Certain types of objections are quite common, so understanding why these objections occur and how to handle them is crucial. Once you've mastered these common objections, you'll be better equipped to deal with unusual ones. And since the first objection a prospect raises is rarely the real issue, you'll need to learn how to drill down until you've uncovered the underlying problem and resolved it.

OBJECTIONS ARE A GOOD THING

Resolving Objections and Moving Forward

Salespeople often dread objections because they see them as obstacles to closing the sale. In reality it's a good sign when prospects raise objections. It means they're interested enough in purchasing to bring up some potential issues and give you a chance to solve them. If the prospect isn't interested at all, she'll just leave.

Conditions versus Objections

A condition is an issue that truly can't be overcome—for instance, a binding contract with one of your competitors. You can and should address your prospect's objections during the sales process. If the prospect raises a condition, however, it's time to throw in the towel.

One of the most difficult things about overcoming objections is that you must do it in a way that shows respect for your prospect. When you respond to an objection, it's often necessary to disagree with what the prospect has just told you. For example, you can't just agree when she says, "Your product is too expensive," or something of that nature! The secret is finding a way to disagree without being confrontational.

The salesperson's instinctive response to such an objection is typically something like, "No, here's why our price isn't too high..." The reason this response is problematic is that it starts by telling the prospect she's wrong. At a minimum this will probably irritate the prospect. At worst she'll just stop listening altogether. In either case she won't be listening too closely to your explanation.

Often, objections are the result of a misunderstanding on the part of the prospect. For example, an objection based on price ("Your product is too expensive") may come from various sources. Maybe she got a much lower price quote from a competitor for a product that appears to be just like yours. Maybe she hasn't priced products in your industry for a number of years and doesn't know that costs have changed significantly. Or maybe she's afraid she can't afford the product and is instinctively blaming your product's price.

Rather than explaining why the prospect is wrong, ask a question that will determine the basis of the objection. Perhaps you could ask something like, "Really? Can you explain what you mean by that?" If she asks what you mean, say, "I want to understand how you came to that conclusion. For example, is it based on a price you saw somewhere?" Her answer will probably clarify the source of the original objection.

Once you have figured out where the objection is coming from—for example, the prospect replies, "This competitor makes exactly the same product for half the price"—you can clear up the objection without annoying your prospect. Responding along the lines of, "That's true, because Company Z's product doesn't have these features," will explain why the prices are different without actually disagreeing with your prospect.

If you can give the customer some alternative choices, that's even better. A response like, "If you don't need the additional features I mentioned, you may be interested in a different version of this product for a lower price," can make the prospect feel that you're taking her issue seriously and can increase her trust in you. It also provides her with more options to choose from. As a result, you're more likely to end up with a new customer.

Another way to resolve objections without being confrontational is to find an approach that will allow you to agree with the prospect. For example, in the case of an objection concerning price, you could say, "I absolutely agree that it's important to have all the information before you invest your money in something, so if it's all right with you, I'll explain why we set that particular price..." and then go into specifics.

Above all, don't begin a presentation before you've armed yourself with plenty of facts. If you don't know why your product costs more than a competitor's product, you can't respond to that objection without being confrontational. Your only option in that situation is to provide vague answers like, "Our product is better, so it costs more." Objections are usually based on the prospect's fears, and responding with a generalization is only going to deepen those fears. But if you have an in-depth understanding of your industry and a solid knowledge of your products, you can support your statements with hard facts, and the prospect will feel much more comfortable trusting in you.

THE "NOT INTERESTED" OBJECTION

If They're Talking, They're Still Interested

Most salespeople get a lot of "Sorry, I'm not interested" responses, particularly when cold calling. In fact, this may be the most common objection of all. "I'm not interested" is usually shorthand for "I just realized you're a salesperson and I don't want to deal with you right now."

In other words, the prospect is not objecting to your sales pitch—in fact, he probably wasn't listening to what you said. He may even have a strong need for your product, but because he was tuning you out, he may not even realize what you're selling. Resolving this objection usually means finding a way to get the prospect to actually pay attention and listen to you.

Not Interested after a Presentation?

Getting "I'm not interested" objections after you've made a sales presentation is a much more worrisome sign than if you run across it while cold calling. It means that you either didn't identify the right need or that the prospect never intended to buy from you.

RESPONSE #1

"What would have to change for you to be interested?"

This response is helpful because it gets the prospect actually thinking about what you're offering, and it may help her make the connection and realize that she really does need your product. If she gives you a real answer to this question, ask her when that's likely to happen and then get her permission to call at that point. If she shuts you out by saying something like, "I'm just not interested," you'll need to try a stronger response or move on to another prospect.

RESPONSE #2

"Do you already own a [product type]?"

If the prospect answers yes to this question, follow up with, "And how do you like that product?" or the equivalent version that works for you. If he answers no, ask something like, "Have you ever wished you did own one?" If he shuts you down again, thank him for his time and file him away with your inactive leads. You can try calling him again in a few weeks and see if you catch him in a better mood.

RESPONSE #3

"Who else in your organization might have a need for [product type]?"

This is a good response to use if you get the sense that the prospect isn't just shutting you down but actually doesn't have a need for your product (or at least believes that she doesn't have a need). With this response you may be able to get a quick referral to the person who really does need to buy from you. If you're selling to consumers rather than businesses, you can use an equivalent response such as, "Who do you know who's currently shopping for [product type]?" Framing the question in an open-ended way instead of asking a yes-or-no question like, "Do you know someone who has a need for [product type]?" makes it more likely that you'll get a positive or at least thoughtful reply.

RESPONSE #4

"I understand. When should I get back to you?"

If the prospect's response to this is "never," you may want to haul out response #1 or #2 to try to get more information. If he gives you a time frame, such as six months from now, pick an actual date and time and reply, "Okay, I'll give you a call back June sixth at ten o'clock if that works for you." Setting a specific appointment to talk with the prospect improves your odds of actually getting a hold of him at that time.

RESPONSE #5

"Okay. Before I quit bugging you, are you the right contact for this or should I speak with someone else at your organization?"

Be sure to smile as you deliver this response; believe it or not, people on the phone can actually hear if you're smiling. You want to add a little lightness to the conversation with this response. Hopefully, you can get a prospect in a slightly more cheerful mood and increase the odds of getting a real answer to this question. If she responds that she is the correct contact, thank her and make a note to give her a call in a few months.

RESPONSE #6

"I'm actually not calling to sell you something today. I just wanted to give you my contact information and let you know that I'm the one to call if you have any questions about [product type]."

This is a great response if you plan to do some lead nurturing on this prospect before you actually start moving him through the sales process. If he responds in an even slightly positive manner, ask him if he'd like to receive your informational newsletter (assuming you have one) and get his email address.

THE "WE ALREADY HAVE ONE" OBJECTION

This One Is Better

It's not unusual when making cold calls for the lead to respond to your opening with "We already have one of those" or "We're talking to another vendor about that already." But if you consider it, that is a pretty meaningless objection. Unless you're selling some kind of newly invented product or service, most prospects will already have a similar product. When you hear this objection from a prospect, it's generally simply because she doesn't want to make waves.

The best way to deal with this objection is to head it off. You can accomplish this by demonstrating to the prospect from the beginning how your product is different. Describing your product's unique selling qualities and including them in your cold call opener gives you a compelling way to get the prospect's attention, and if your unique selling proposition (USP) is truly unique, she can hardly say that she already has one of those.

Gatekeepers will often employ the "We already have one" objection as a way to get you off the phone. Usually the gatekeeper doesn't know how his boss feels about their current supplier; he's just making an effort to protect the boss from another annoying salesperson.

In this case don't try to pitch your product to the gatekeeper, because you would just be wasting your time. Instead, thank him, hang up, and try to reach the decision-maker directly at another time. Be aware that gatekeepers are far less likely to block you if you ask for the decision-maker by name, rather than asking who is responsible for a specific purchase. Doing a little research to determine the decision-maker's name before you call can save you a lot of time and effort during the call itself.

Like gatekeepers, decision-makers use this objection to get you off the phone. In that case they probably have no idea whether or not your product is different or better than their current purchase; they simply don't want to consider the possibility of change.

POSSIBLE RESPONSES

This objection is similar to the "I'm not interested" objection, and many of the responses for that objection will work well for this one. Other responses that you can use include:

- **"That's a great product. In fact, many of my customers tell me that it's compatible with ours."** With this response, you're implying that the prospect could benefit from owning both versions of the product. Needless to say, you'd better have facts to back up your assertion.
- **"What do you like best about the product?"** This response tackles the objection from a slightly sneaky direction. Prospects will expect you to ask what they don't like about the competing product, but they won't expect you to ask for praise. Unexpected questions can do an excellent job of jarring prospects out of their resistance and getting them to actually listen to you.
- **"How long have you owned the product?"** The answer to this question will give you insight into what their pain points might be. If the prospect has owned a competing product for years or decades, his model is likely to be outdated and not as full-featured as whatever you're selling. If he just bought it recently,

on the other hand, he's not necessarily wedded to it, and whatever implementation hassles he suffered are fresh in his mind.

Sometimes finding and clarifying pain points can jar the prospect into listening to you. If that doesn't work, you will probably have to put the sales process on hold and come back to that prospect at a later date. You can use the time in between to build rapport with the prospect by sending him useful information, getting to know him better, finding common interests and acquaintances, and so on. When you reconnect with him later to try again, he'll be far more likely to listen with an open mind.

Battling Inertia

The toughest competitor every salesperson faces is the status quo. Most people are uncomfortable with change, so even if they aren't crazy about their current product, they may cling to it rather than buy another.

Salespeople also frequently hear this objection or a variant of it after a sales presentation. This usually means that the prospect isn't convinced that your product is an improvement over his existing one. The best way to handle the objection in this case is to step back and collect some more information from him.

You might use one of the previously mentioned responses or say something general, like, "Can you tell me a little more about your [current model/current supplier/current adviser]?" Then listen carefully to uncover any hints of dissatisfaction. It's quite likely that there are a few things the prospect doesn't like about his provider, but he'd rather put up with those minor problems than go through the pain of switching. You may be able to draw out those pain points and show him that it would indeed be a good value to buy your product instead.

Sometimes companies will put together websites or white papers that compare their products with the top competitors. Check with your marketing department to see if they have something like that already prepared, and if they don't, urge them to create one. It can be an excellent resource for resolving this objection, as well as a good handout for prospects.

THE "I JUST BOUGHT FROM YOUR COMPETITOR" OBJECTION

Keep Things Open for the Future

This objection is one that salespeople tend to find particularly daunting. After all, if the prospect just bought a different version of the product last week, there's no way she'd buy another one today, right? But "I just bought from your competitor," like all objections, is not necessarily the end of the line. If you keep your cool and take the right steps, you may be able to overcome it and keep the sale moving forward.

The natural reaction to this objection is to get upset about your terrible timing, but if you do get upset, it will significantly decrease your chances of handling the objection appropriately. Don't start berating yourself for not having called this prospect a week ago, and definitely don't get hostile toward the prospect. Shelve your anger and frustration and stay calm, so that you can start finding out what you need to know.

Objection Timing

You generally won't hear this objection after a sales presentation, since if the prospect has bought from a competitor, she's not likely to show up for the appointment. More often you'll hear it either on a cold call or when a prospect calls to cancel an appointment.

Find out exactly what the prospect means by "bought." That might seem pretty obvious, but some prospects will say they've bought from a competitor when they are actually still in the middle of the buying process. Or they may have decided to buy from the other company but haven't actually committed to the deal or signed a contract. In these cases you may be able to sneak in and snatch away the sale from your competitor.

How much effort you're willing to put in at this point will depend on how valuable the prospect is. For a really significant prospect, it may be worth dropping everything and driving over to her office right then and there to make a presentation (assuming she agrees to this, of course). Being willing to make such a gesture with zero notice should score you some points with that prospect. If the prospect is not quite as far along in the competitor's buying process, you may be able to set up an appointment within the next few days to hopefully win her over.

If the prospect confirms that she has in fact sealed a deal with your competitor, then you have lost the chance to make a sale—for now. However, that doesn't mean you've lost the prospect. It's entirely possible that a few months from now this prospect will once again be in the market, and if you can nurture her and impress her during the intervening period, she'll give you a shot at the sale. That's one reason why staying calm and pleasant is so important in this situation. Try one of the following responses:

- **"Thank you for clarifying. When does your contract expire?"** Make a note to call the prospect again a few weeks before that contract runs out.
- **"I'm familiar with that product. Have you had any trouble with [common product issue]?"** You can drop in any issue that a

customer has complained about or that you've heard about from multiple sources. Trolling forums, social media networks, and reviews will give you ample examples of such product issues.

- **"I hope the product meets your needs. Do I have your permission to contact you in one month and see how things are going with you?"** If the prospect ends up unhappy with her purchase, this one-month checkup can give you a great opportunity to convince her to buy a replacement product from you.

If all of this fails and you lose the prospect for all time, you can still wring some benefit out of the situation by mining the prospect for details. Find out why she bought from that particular competitor instead of from you or from some other company. If you can, find out what research the prospect did before buying, what her buying process entailed, and what the competitor did to win her over. Also try to find out how the prospect feels about your company and your product lines. Again, the nicer you are, the more likely the prospect will be to give you this kind of information. It's basic human nature to feel guilty when you reject someone and the rejected party is really nice about it.

If you start hearing a *lot* of prospects telling you that they've just bought from one particular competitor, you'll definitely want to find out what's going on. Is that company running some kind of special offer or promotion? Have they just hired a huge number of salespeople who are swarming all over your territory? Have they launched a brand-new marketing campaign? Do they have a new product that they are really pushing, and if so, how do its features and benefits stack up against those of your own products? The more you know about this competitor, the better your chances of winning some of those prospects back over to you.

THE "THAT'S TOO EXPENSIVE" OBJECTION

The Danger of Discounting

Price objections are one of the most common objections that salespeople hear. A price objection can take a number of different forms: "That's too expensive," "Your competitor's product is cheaper," "I can't afford that," and so on. All of these objections are ways for the prospect to push back on cost.

Many prospects will automatically object and ask for a discount regardless of how they feel about the price of a particular product or service. Many salespeople will just as automatically offer an immediate discount.

Discounting on price is almost always a bad idea. First, that discount comes straight out of the sale's profit margin. Second, offering a discount gives the prospect the impression that you were overcharging with your initial price. Third, once you discount on a purchase, you will find it very difficult to avoid offering discounts on all future purchases that that prospect makes. And fourth, prospects who are interested in price above all other details are usually very difficult customers.

Any product or service is like a three-legged stool, and the legs are quality, service, and price. If you lower one leg—say, you lower the price of a product—then the other two legs have to go down as well. You'll have to reduce quality and service to pay for that price reduction, or your company won't be able to afford to offer the product. Salespeople who have a habit of offering discounts fail to take this into consideration. In extreme cases such salespeople have discounted their companies right into bankruptcy.

So how do you close the sale without caving on a prospect's price objection? First of all, price is rarely the most important factor in a prospect's decision to buy. In fact, most prospects who are considering different products at a range of prices will choose one of the middle options rather than the cheapest, unless they have a compelling reason to do otherwise. People are well aware that you get what you pay for and will automatically assume that there's something wrong with the cheapest available product.

Hold Off on Talking Price

Some prospects will ask you about pricing right away, during the initial cold call. Stall them by saying you need more information before you can talk costs. If pressed, give a range of potential prices. It's much easier to deal with price issues after you've talked value.

If you harbor secret doubts that your product is worth the cost, talk to the people in other departments of your company—engineering, customer support, and marketing. Your product may have a value that you never realized, and knowing that value will give a huge boost to your sales efforts. On the other hand, if your research confirms that the product is truly overpriced, it's time to start looking for a sales job elsewhere.

Once you're comfortable with your product's price, you can feel better about defending that price to your prospects. The best way to deal with a price objection is by never letting it come up. When a prospect gives a price objection, it's often because the value he perceives doesn't equal the price you quoted. If you emphasize the product's value during your sales presentation and give several benefits that match the prospect's biggest needs, he'll likely have no trouble matching the value to the price.

WHAT MATTERS TO THE PROSPECT?

To nail down a sale, all you have to do is find out which need or factor is most important to that prospect, and then do everything you can to address that need. For example, one prospect might consider reliability to be the most important benefit when buying a piece of equipment. In that case you might offer to throw in an extended warranty or maintenance plan along with the purchase.

How is this different from offering a discount? For one thing, it's possible that your customer will never use the extended warranty and will never need extra maintenance. In that case it's costing your company nothing. If the customer does use them, such services probably cost your company a lot less than cutting out the profit margin on a purchase. Finally, you've upheld the "sticker price" on the purchase, so when your customer makes future purchases, he won't automatically expect a price cut.

The trick is to find out what concessions your prospect will find most valuable. Often the things that a prospect values highly are things that cost your company very little to provide. In those situations you can really wow the prospect without doing any damage to your profit margin.

Finding out these value points is a necessary part of the sales process anyway, and it generally starts before you ever make your sales presentation. After all, if you don't know what your prospect considers important, how would you know which points to emphasize in your presentation? Then you can simply apply the same points to the negotiation.

On rare occasions you'll run into a prospect who truly does value price above everything else. Such a prospect will usually turn down any concessions you try to make and insist on a discount. In that situation simply tell the prospect that the price you've already offered is in fact your best possible price, and if it's unacceptable, then you're sorry that you weren't able to come to an agreement with him. Then shake his hand and leave. You may have lost the sale, but you've saved yourself from being stuck with a high-maintenance, penny-pinching customer.

THE "I NEED TO THINK ABOUT IT" OBJECTION

Take Away the Fear

It's not uncommon to hear a prospect say, "I need to think about this," or "Let me think about it and get back to you," just when you're about to close the sale. These are commonly known as delaying or time objections. Usually one of two things is happening—either the prospect is considering your offer but needs time to do some other things before he's ready to buy, or he has no intention of buying your product and just wants to get out of there. That means the first step in dealing with this objection is finding out if the prospect is even considering the purchase.

Start by asking for clarification. For example, you might say, "Certainly. Can you tell me more about what's holding you back?" At this point either the prospect will give you more details, such as admitting that he's not the only decision-maker and needs to get approval, or he'll say something vague, like, "I just need to think about the options." The latter response is a bad sign, because it means there's something else going on that he doesn't want you to know about.

Savvy buyers will sometimes use time objections to deliberately stretch out the sales process in order to gain a negotiating advantage. This is especially true of professional buyers, whose job is basically to get the best possible deal for their companies. These prospects will drag their feet deliberately in an attempt to throw you into a panic, so you'll be willing to offer them a better deal.

The key to overcoming time objections is to inject a little urgency into the prospect. Sometimes prospects won't realize how serious their need is until you point it out to them. If you've done your home-work and asked the right questions, you'll have a pretty clear under-standing of the issue that's brought them to speak with you. It may be enough just to rephrase those needs back to them, along with the potential consequences of not fixing the problem. If that doesn't do the trick, it's time to start talking benefits and remind them of what they stand to gain as well.

If a prospect digs in his heels and refuses to move forward, don't try to force him onward. Whether he's doing it to provoke you or out of his own concerns, the best way to handle the situation is to let him take whatever time he needs. Present a calm and confident demeanor and let him know you're there for him with whatever information he needs to make his decision. This will reassure the frightened prospect, and show the savvy prospect that you won't let him panic you.

Usually, once you stop pushing, your prospect will start moving forward again on his own initiative. In fact, there's a school of thought that believes that the slower you sell, the faster the sales process will go. This theory argues that it's pressure from salespeople that trig-gers prospect fears, and if you let things proceed at the prospect's own pace, you'll actually end up selling faster than if you had to spend the time allaying all those fears.

Speeding Up Through Slowing Down

For more information about how letting up on prospects can speed up the sales process, check out *Slow Down, Sell Faster!* by Kevin Davis. This book provides step-by-step guidance for using a low-pressure sales approach.

In fact, fear is the number-one reason why prospects try to delay a purchase. Any change that occurs in someone's life has an element of risk, and buying your product is definitely a change for them. The more a prospect has invested in a purchase, the higher the risk.

Risk in buying relates to the potential costs that a customer may have to pay for your product (and that's not just monetary cost). For example, if he buys a used car from you and brags about what a great deal it was to all his friends, only to discover that the car breaks down constantly, he'll suffer an emotional cost in embarrassment and frustration on top of the money he'll pay for all those repairs.

The first step in reducing that feeling of risk is to help the prospect to trust you personally. Building rapport is an important part of sales because it's the beginning of trust, and if the prospect trusts you, he'll feel better about taking your advice to buy your product.

Another way to reduce a prospect's perception of risk is to demonstrate exactly how he stands to gain more than he stands to lose. Don't just *tell* him about the benefits; *show* him. You might bring a product model to his office and let him try it out, or tell stories about your existing customers and the specific benefits they gained from their purchases.

Bringing "proof" to your appointment is a great way to make the prospect feel safer. Customer testimonials and/or references are very handy. Safety nets, like extended warranties and free maintenance, are also helpful. With a little research, you may be able to get your hands on third-party documents, like case studies, news stories, industry reports, surveys, and so on, to provide further backup. The more support you can show for your product, the less worried prospects will be about buying it.

RESOLVING THE REAL OBJECTION

Whatever the prospect's motives for raising an objection, the issue that she's chosen to express is rarely the issue that she is really concerned about. In fact, a prospect's first objection is often a red herring to draw you away from the real issue.

She might have several different reasons for wanting to keep the truth from you: she might not trust you enough, she might be somewhat embarrassed about the real issue, or she might even be angling for a negotiating advantage. If you're to keep the sales process on track, you'll need to uncover the prospect's true concerns.

The first step toward finding out what's really bugging the prospect is building a rapport with her. If she doesn't trust you, she is unlikely to be completely honest with you. Why would she? Would you talk about your concerns with some nosy stranger you didn't particularly like? Of course not. If you can show the prospect that it's safe to trust you, you'll be much closer to uncovering the real problem.

Building rapport will also help if the prospect is hiding the real problem because she's embarrassed by it. For example, if a prospect feels that she can't afford your product, she may feel bad about that and not exactly inclined to talk about it at great length. If she starts feeling that she can trust you, however, she may be willing to open up about it.

What Is Rapport?

Rapport is a positive emotional connection that includes feelings of trust. Successfully building rapport with your prospects and customers is the key to having long, lucrative relationships with them. Since most people don't trust salespeople, it can be quite a challenge.

Once you've made a connection with the prospect, she may volunteer her real concern—but it's more likely that you'll still have to dig for the truth. Usually you can get at the truth simply by asking questions about the objection that the prospect has raised. For example, if the objection is "This isn't a good time," you can ask questions like, "What makes this a bad time for you?" or "Why do you feel this isn't a good time?" If the prospect throws out a vague-sounding response, like, "I'm just really busy right now," continue to press for more information. "Why" questions are often particularly useful in uncovering the truth behind an objection.

It's important to go through this information-gathering procedure with objections because if you simply take the prospect objection at face value and try to resolve it, you'll be addressing a concern that doesn't really matter to the prospect. Whatever you say at this point, you won't be resolving the issue that's really holding her back. Resolving the wrong objection will usually result in a brush-off, like, "I'll think about it and talk to you later." If you leave it at that, don't bother waiting by the phone for her call.

Once you've gone through a layer or two of questions and feel that you've uncovered the true objection, you can start working with the prospect to resolve it. At this point asking more questions can be very helpful because it helps you to settle the issue without seeming to lecture the prospect or making her look foolish.

For example, if the prospect finally admits that she is really concerned about being able to afford your product, you can ask her questions to uncover how much she'd be comfortable spending, and whether her cash flow issues are temporary or permanent. If it's a temporary shortage, perhaps setting her up with a payment plan would suffice to get her back on track and ready to buy. Using this approach, you can close the sale and earn the prospect's gratitude at the same time.

Is the Sale Dead?

Sometimes, no matter what you say or do, the prospect will just keep throwing out objections. That's a definite warning sign that he doesn't intend to buy from you, and the sale is officially dead. The only way to find out for sure is to ask the prospect some tough questions.

A mistake many salespeople make is phrasing questions as though you expect a positive answer. If you say something like, "Everything's okay on your end, right?" or "Are we still probably going to finalize the purchase by the end of this month?" you're making it easy for the prospect to evade issues by simply saying, "Yes, we're fine," and leaving it at that. When problems do arise, prospects are often hesitant to bring them up because they don't want to deliver the bad news.

For instance, if your prospect raised a price objection during your initial presentation, when you follow up you might want to ask something like, "So are there any remaining concerns that you have about price?" If you ask for feedback, you're much more likely to get an honest response than if you say, "We're all set on price now, right?"

When you phrase a question so that it invites a negative response rather than a positive one, one of two things will happen. Either the prospect will admit that in fact there is a problem, or he will say that everything is fine. If he admits that there is a problem, you have an opportunity to fix it before your prospect does something that can't be changed, like buying from another vendor. If he says there's no problem, you can feel more confident that he's being honest because you gave him a true opportunity to communicate his feelings.

It can be scary asking such tough questions, but doing so provides an important benefit: you get to clear dead sales out of your pipeline rather than living in foolish optimism about how many sales you have pending.

CHAPTER 6
CLOSING THE SALE

By the time you reach the close, you're in the home stretch on that sale. How you handle the close will determine whether or not you get the sale—it's your last chance, so don't blow it! Before you reach that point, laying the right groundwork will help ensure that things will go your way. The better you do at building rapport, creating urgency, and uncovering needs during the earlier parts of the sales cycle, the easier the close will be. Approaching closing with a confident attitude is another key component of success. Your confidence helps prospects feel more confident too. Once you actually start closing, you can use closing techniques to help nudge difficult prospects into making the right decision. However, these techniques should be used with caution and only when necessary. Finally, closing stalled sales requires a special approach, but when done right it can rescue sales that you'd long since given up on.

WHAT IS CLOSING?

The Goal of the Sale

In sales terms, closing refers to the moment when a prospect decides to go ahead with the purchase. The problem is, unless the prospect is extremely eager to buy today, he'll rarely decide to do so after a sales presentation. It's much more natural to take some time to think things over and maybe do a bit more research.

Of course, once the prospect leaves the sales appointment, you lose any chance to influence her decision. That's why it's so important to close prospects while you have them in front of you. If a prospect has any unrevealed concerns or hesitations, these will come out at the close—and you may be able to resolve them on the spot and walk away with a sale. Fortunately, closing a sale can be quite a simple and basic process.

If you've done a good job in the early stages of the sales process, you'll have very little to do to get the sale closed. In that case the close could be as simple as saying, "Sign on the dotted line to make it yours," while giving the prospect a pen and a blank contract.

Trial Closes

You don't have to wait until the very end to use a trial close. During your sales presentation a trial close can help you to flush out any prospect concerns while you still have plenty of time to address them.

Closing tends to become complicated when your prospect isn't really ready to buy after your sales presentation ends. You can generally tell how the prospect is feeling by watching out for buying signals. If her body language is tense or closed up as you're coming to the end of your presentation, she's probably not convinced that it's time to buy.

In that case it can be helpful to do a trial close before you push onward to a final close. A trial close tests the prospect's readiness to buy. A basic trial close could sound something like, "Is there any reason you wouldn't want to put in an order here and now?"

A prospect who isn't ready to buy will often respond to a trial close by tossing out an objection. If you respond appropriately to the objection she mentions, she'll come up with another one and possibly yet another one. Remember that objections are actually a good sign because if the prospect is truly not interested, she'll just say no thanks and walk out the door. Objections at this point in the process are more like yellow flags: the prospect is trying to slow down the buying process until she feels more comfortable with the idea.

Once you've responded to all of the prospect's post-trial-close objections, you can either float another trial close or head right into your final close, depending on how confident the prospect seems at that point. This is generally a make-it-or-break-it point for that sale. Once the prospect has run out of objections, she'll give you a firm yes or no.

CONVERTING A "NO" TO A "YES"

A no after an attempted close is not necessarily the end of all your hopes. Depending on the prospect's reasons for saying no, you still might be able to change his mind. If he sticks to his no, you can reach out to him at a later date when he has more of a need for what you're selling.

Salespeople have come up with a variety of closing techniques to help soften a prospect's resistance and put him in a buying mood. These closing techniques can be quite powerful and blatant and should be used only when necessary. You should never use a closing technique to coerce a prospect into buying something that he doesn't truly want or need. Closing techniques are best used when the prospect is nearly ready to buy but is held back by some minor concern—most often fear of making a mistake.

The typical salesperson's attitude toward closing and closing techniques has changed quite a bit since the days of *Glengarry Glen Ross*. Most salespeople view the close as the chance to provide a prospect with something that will improve his life in some way. As a result, hard closes are much less popular these days than they once were. In fact, some salespeople have moved so far toward a softer selling approach that they believe *all* closing is inappropriate. In reality, though, some form of a close is a necessity for almost every sale.

BEFORE YOU CLOSE THE SALE

A salesperson's job boils down to convincing prospects that they are better off with the product than they are without it. If you do this successfully during the first stages of the sales process, then the close will happen naturally. But if you fail to prove the product's benefits to your prospect, closing will be an uphill struggle. You'll find yourself in the position of closing *and* responding to objections *and* presenting your product all at once. No wonder salespeople have trouble closing in these conditions!

Salespeople look for customer touchpoints. These may be the customer seeing the product in a store, but more often they're a customer interaction with the product through the company's website, a digital ad, or an online interaction. Such touchpoints are jumping-off places for the salesperson's pitch, since the customer now knows the basic facts about the product and what problems it can solve for him or her.

Trade shows are significant touchpoints where consumers can encounter a product, often for the first time. Interactions at trade shows can generate leads, so the salesperson can follow up with "warm calling" in order to get an appointment to move the sale along.

The basic skills of selling have remained essentially the same from decade to decade: know the product, identify the customer's needs, and show how your product can meet those needs. Even though door-to-door salespeople are less prevalent with the growth of the Internet and social media, today's salespeople can learn from their example of how to pitch and how to close a sale.

Some companies—Young Living, Thirty-One Gifts, and others—recruit their own customers to become salespeople. Representatives hold gatherings at their homes and invite their friends to listen to their sales pitch for the company's product. The representatives, in return, receive a commission on sales.

Photo Credit: © Getty Images/jacoblund

John Henry Patterson (1844–1922), together with his brother, formed the National Cash Register Company in 1884. Besides innovating in business practices (such as building a factory with large windows and plenty of fresh air), he created a sales training school, the first of its kind. His catchphrase was, "We cannot afford to have a single dissatisfied customer."

Napoleon Hill (1883–1970) was a bestselling self-help author. His philosophy that success is best achieved through working harmoniously with others was widely adopted by salespeople. They applied his principles to working in cooperation with the customer to resolve challenges the customer was trying to solve.

Today, many salespeople no longer simply cold call, but combine cold calling with cold emailing. Finding a strategy that uses both means of communication increases the chances of reaching the prospect. But whatever the case, the goal remains the same: don't worry about getting a sale; get an appointment.

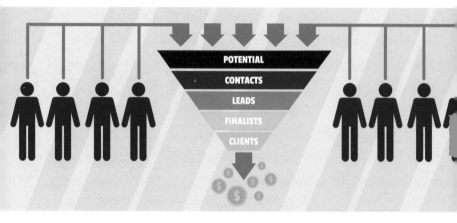

It's important to understand and qualify prospects no matter where they fall in the prospecting funnel. This is one of the objectives of the sales appointment: to gather information about the prospect's needs, the structure of his or her organization, who the decision-makers are, and so on. Using that information, the salesperson can move the prospect to the next stage of the sales cycle.

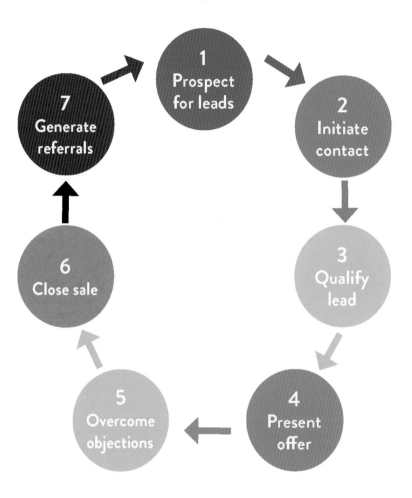

The basic form of a sales cycle has seven components. Each of these leads logically into the next, ending in referrals, which create opportunities to begin the cycle all over again.

Photo Credit: © Simon & Schuster, Inc.

Successful salespeople listen to their customers and ask questions. They often use the Socratic method, first developed more than 2,500 years ago by the Greek philosopher Socrates (shown here). In ancient Athens, Socrates developed the method of leading someone, through questions, to draw his or her own conclusions.

Before you can start closing, you've got to check that you have indeed convinced the prospect of the benefits to come from owning your product. And they can't be just any benefits; you must match the benefits to the prospect's specific needs or you'll be wasting your time (and the prospect's). If a prospect wants something that will speed up his manufacturing process and all you've been talking about is how cheap your product is, you won't have much luck closing him.

Before you start talking about benefits you must be sure that you understand the prospect's hot-button needs. Ideally, you should uncover at least three important needs and a few less important ones. Why so many? Because first, the more needs you know about, the better you can target your benefits statements; second, you may be wrong about the importance of one of those needs, so having others to target will ensure that you're discussing at least one critical prospect need; and third, your product may not be particularly attuned to one of the prospect's needs, but if it can meet two other important needs, then you still have some solid benefits to offer the prospect.

Once you've asked the right questions and uncovered the prospect's needs, you've got to match those needs to the product's benefits. Since you'll almost certainly have to do this on the fly, you'd better know your product very well before you ever arrive at the appointment. Sometimes you'll be able to uncover a need or two early in the sales process and you can prepare your benefits statements in advance, but more often the needs-uncovering phase and the benefit-explaining phase will both happen in a single appointment.

Competitive Research

Studying up on the competition can be useful at many stages of the sales process. See if your sales manager will pay for you to buy competing products and get familiar with them. If not, sign up for demos while pretending to be a prospect.

It's also wise to study your competitors' products, because many times prospects will either ask how your models stack up or bring up a specific feature that competing products have and yours doesn't. This is especially likely if your prospect currently owns one of those competing products. If you can clearly explain how your product will meet the prospect's needs as well as or better than anything else out there, you've got a much better shot at landing the sale.

Explaining your product's benefits isn't the end of the process either. Just because you mentioned a benefit doesn't necessarily mean that the prospect understands why that benefit is important for her. Before you head into the close, you've got to verify the prospect's level of understanding. This is easily accomplished by asking a series of open-ended questions. For example, if your prospect disclosed her need to speed up the assembly line and you then brought up the product's ability to save manufacturing time because of its excellent reliability, you could pause and say, "Does that make sense?" or "How does that sound to you?" The prospect's answer will give you a good idea of whether she relates to the benefit you've just described.

If you've successfully matched benefits to needs and confirmed that the prospect agrees with your viewpoint, the close should be a slam dunk. You can test the waters by using a trial close like, "Okay, let's get this order in today and you can have it running on your assembly line by Tuesday." If the prospect pushes back at this point, you missed a step somewhere. Either your need/benefit combination isn't compelling enough to spur immediate action, or there's a problem you didn't uncover yet. In that case it's time to step back to an earlier stage of the sales cycle and figure out where you went wrong.

For example, you might want to go all the way back to the qualifying phase and ask your prospect some questions to try to narrow down what she really needs. Or you might switch back into presentation mode to spell out just how the product can benefit your prospect. The challenge at this point is to zip through these repeated stages as quickly as possible, since you've already taken up a lot of your prospect's time. Eventually her patience will wear out and you'll lose any chance of closing—perhaps forever, if she's really annoyed with you.

HOW TO CLOSE WITH CONFIDENCE

Confidence Is Contagious

Closing the sale can be an anxiety-producing moment for salespeople at all levels of experience. It's often the do-or-die moment for a sale, and on top of that, closing, like cold calling, opens up the possibility for rejection.

But closing doesn't have to be a frightening moment. If you go into the close feeling confident that the prospect is ready to buy, you'll have a much lower anxiety level. Closing with confidence will also improve your odds because that confidence is infectious. Prospects will pick up on that feeling and will be more inclined to believe you know what you're talking about when you tell them how happy the product will make them.

First, remember the cardinal rule of closing—the better your sales presentation is, the easier your close will be. Having a better sales presentation does not correlate to a slick presentation slide deck or lots of fancy brochures. It means that your sales presentation has correctly identified the prospect's needs and presented compelling evidence that your product will meet those needs. If you've accomplished that important task during your appointment, the close can be nothing more than your saying, "Sign on the dotted line."

The trouble is that not every sale will go so smoothly. You may miss hints from the prospect that cause you to focus on how the product will serve all the wrong needs, or there may be other issues you didn't pick up on. Any obstacles you didn't remove during your sales presentation will block you from closing the sale.

When closing, it's also crucial to identify the perfect moment when the prospect is not only ready but also eager to buy. The close that would be greeted enthusiastically at one moment can be turned down flat fifteen minutes later, after the prospect has had time to entertain second thoughts. Fortunately, most prospects will send strong signals when they're ready to buy; all you have to do is learn to read them.

RECOGNIZING BUYING SIGNALS

Buying signals are your indicator that it's time to start closing. Common buying signals include the prospect leaning forward toward you, suddenly relaxing back in his chair, smiling and nodding in response to the points that you make during the presentation, and asking questions that imply that the prospect has already made the purchase in his mind, such as "Do you have the red one in stock?"

Body Language

Understanding body language is a huge advantage for salespeople. Canny prospects will do their best to hide their feelings. If you can read what's going on underneath, you'll know just what to do to cinch the sale.

If you're not sure if the prospect is ready to buy, you can float a trial close like, "If I can get you this product in red today, are you ready to buy right now?" If the prospect replies with a definite yes, move on to the real close. If he says no or seems uncertain, you have some more obstacle-removing work to do first.

Buying signals and trial closes don't just help you spot the right moment. They also give you confidence as you head into the close, and that feeling of confidence will have two important positive results. First, it will make you feel safer about presenting the close. Many a junior salesperson leaves an appointment without ever closing and loses an easy sale as a result. If you feel confident about closing, you won't make that particular mistake. Second, your confidence can help the prospect get over his own nervousness about making the purchase and will make him happier about buying.

When you start the close, you'll often get an objection or three from the prospect. Some salespeople interpret these objections as a rejection or refusal to buy. In reality, objections just mean that the prospect feels he doesn't know enough yet to make a decision, or that he doesn't think it's urgent.

If your prospect objects at the close, ask some careful questions to figure out which of these two problems is holding him back. In the first case you've got to find out just what the prospect needs to know to feel ready to buy, and then get him that information. In the second case you'll need to uncover more about the problem that led him to attend your sales presentation, and then explain all the wonderful ways that owning this product will resolve that problem and make his life better.

USING CLOSING TECHNIQUES

If All Else Fails...

The rule of thumb in any sale is that the better you do during the sales process, the easier it is to close the customer. If you've gotten to the end of your presentation and haven't convinced the prospect to buy, you're going to have a tough time closing. On the other hand, if you've done a good job of building rapport and outlining benefits, your close might be as simple as asking the prospect to sign on the dotted line.

Some salespeople have no trouble using closing techniques and find them quite effective. They start closing right at the beginning of the appointment, using a statement like, "If I show you how this product will save you seventy-five percent over your current product, will you buy today?" and go on from there. But these salespeople are successful because they're using social psychology tricks to manipulate the prospect into buying. Closing techniques work by pressuring people into feeling that they must make the purchase; in the short term, they generate sales, but in the long term those customers may feel resentful.

Closing Techniques for New Salespeople

If you're new to sales, stick with basic closing statements with perhaps the addition of one or two very simple closing techniques. The more elaborate techniques require the ability to read prospects, deliver statements convincingly, and have perfect timing. You'll need some experience to gain the necessary skills.

Other salespeople detest closing techniques, insisting that any salesperson who resorts to the traditional closes isn't doing a good job of selling. But it's rare for a sales process to go so well that you will have no need to close at all. If you build sufficient rapport with a prospect and find a product that does a great job of meeting her needs, then she'll be quite easy to close. Even so, most prospects won't buy from you immediately unless you give them a little push (or a big one).

The salesperson's biggest enemy is inertia, which is why closing techniques can come in very handy. Change is a frightening thing, and unless they have a compelling reason to do otherwise, prospects will stay with "the devil they know" rather than taking a risk by buying something new. So even if you've made an effective pitch and the prospect actually believes your product is the best option, if you don't nudge him by closing the sale, he's most likely going to put off actually buying from you until he feels he has to. The bigger the change and the more expensive the purchase, the more likely it is that prospects will delay things as long as they can.

The proper use of closing techniques, then, is to give the last little push that gets your prospect moving. Each previous stage in the sales process should ideally contribute to making the prospect feel that buying your product is going to be much better than leaving things as they are. Star salespeople can usually stick with very simple closing techniques because they're careful to lay the appropriate groundwork during the presentation.

For example, one simple yet powerful closing technique is known as the presumptive close. With this approach, you make a statement or ask a question that presumes that the prospect intends to buy from you. If your prospect is on the fence, this assumption may be enough to push her into buying.

PRESUMPTIVE CLOSE QUESTIONS AND STATEMENTS

Presumptive close questions and statements sound like this:

- "Would you rather have the green one or the yellow one?"
- "With standard delivery, the unit will arrive in three days. Will you need priority delivery, or will that be sufficient?"
- "If you're willing to pay in advance, I can apply a ten percent prepayment discount to your order. Would you like to go ahead with that?"

The more complicated closing techniques are typically "harder" in both senses of the word. They're harder because they're more difficult to pull off, but they're also hard-sell methods. These closing techniques work by pressuring the prospect into a buying decision that he's not ready to make on his own initiative. Most salespeople get better results with simple closes than with trickier ones.

Sometimes a sale is all but lost by the time you reach the close. This may be due to a mistake you made, or it may have nothing to do with you. If your prospect happens to be having a really bad day, he'll be much tougher to sell to no matter how well you deliver your presentation. In these situations a complex close can resuscitate a sale that would otherwise be a total loss.

One of the biggest risks of complex closes is that they're likely to annoy the prospect unless you deliver them just right, since, unlike basic closes, they are pretty blatant. But if the prospect is obviously not planning on making a purchase, an advanced closing technique can sometimes turn things around at the last minute.

The "lost cause" close is a good example of how this works. If your prospect makes it clear through his body language and noncommittal comments that he's not exactly impressed with your sales pitch, then trying a traditional close will result in either a "no, thanks" from the prospect or a stalling objection.

So instead of trying to close the prospect in the normal manner, say something like, "I'm sorry, but it's clear that I made a mistake in coming to talk to you today. I don't think this product is right for you, so I won't waste any more of your time." Pick up your things, shake the prospect's hand and wish him luck, and start heading for the door.

A reaction like this on your part, which is exactly the opposite of what the prospect is expecting, can be enough to jar him out of his closed mindset and might just make him stop you on the way out the door. Or...it might not. That's why this particular closing technique is best used when you're pretty sure the sale is lost otherwise.

CLOSING A STALLED SALE

Kicking the Prospect Back Into Gear

Every salesperson has at least a few stalled sales clogging up the works. These sales involve prospects who are initially enthusiastic about the product, yet somehow they never get around to making a buying decision. Calls and emails to the prospects have no effect, although if you can actually get them on the phone, they will still insist they're interested. Most of these stalled sales happen because the prospects haven't made up their minds to take the plunge.

Often these prospects are interested in buying from you, but they don't want to take the time to do research or to complete the buying process. Like everyone else today, they're busy people trying to balance a lot of tasks, and talking to you keeps sliding down their to-do list because it's replaced by higher-priority tasks.

KICK-STARTING A STALLED SALE

Most stalled sales can be kick-started by raising the prospect's level of urgency. The trick is to show the prospect that this purchase actually is a high priority, and she must take the time to get it done or face serious consequences. You can link the purchase to either a positive need (e.g., your product will help her achieve something important) or a negative one (e.g., your product will fix a serious problem that she's been trying to solve).

Before you try to meet with the prospect again, you'll need to do some research. Look over the information you collected during your original appointment, and toss in everything you can find online and on social media about your prospect. If you're lucky, all that information will give you a better idea of her needs.

Getting another meeting with the prospect will probably be a challenge. Try leaving a few tantalizing hints on her voicemail or in an email about the solutions that your research uncovered, and if you're right about her needs, she'll be perfectly willing to see you again.

Researching Prospect Needs

Checking out social media is a great way to identify prospect needs. For example, if a prospect announces a new baby on *Facebook*, you can congratulate the prospect at your meeting (building rapport) and then tie in your product with creating financial security (which will resonate with a new parent). Don't overdo this approach, though, lest you make the prospect feel like she's being stalked. For example, you might focus your pitch on financial security without spelling out why you chose that tack.

In order to create that feeling of urgency, you must figure out which needs are the most important to the prospect. You'll uncover those needs by asking the right questions and getting her talking. As she discusses the need you bring up, watch her body language—you'll often be able to tell which issues are bothering her the most by the way she squirms or acts uncomfortable while talking about them.

At this point you should start asking anxiety-provoking questions to get her thinking. Simply telling a prospect why a specific issue is serious won't necessarily get her thinking, but if you phrase your concern in the form of a question, she will automatically visualize the scenario you're asking about, and it will have far more of an impact on her.

For example, if your prospect's expressed need is that she must raise her department's productivity by 15 percent by the end of the year, you might ask something like, "What will happen if you don't raise your productivity as needed?" or "What if you run out of time?" Another approach is to say, "How has your current setup affected the productivity issue you're now experiencing?" These questions both generate anxiety in your prospect and get her thinking about how to solve the problem—and what might happen if she fails!

Now that you've increased her sense of urgency, talk your prospect through how your product can resolve her need. Since she'll probably be feeling quite worried by now, benefits terms such as *peace of mind*, *security*, *convenience*, *safety*, and so on will be particularly effective.

Next, float out a trial close to see if she's ready to make a decision. You can say something like, "So how does that sound so far?" and see how she reacts. If she responds with a stall, like, "I need to think about it more," or "I'm not ready to buy now; call me next month," it means she doesn't feel enough urgency yet to buy.

If despite your best efforts you still can't get her moving, then it's time for you to be moving on. After a certain point a sale is no longer worth pursuing, because you're spending so much time and energy on it. Make a note to give her a call in a few months when her need may have become more urgent.

CHAPTER 7
ASKING FOR REFERRALS

The final stage of the sales cycle is not when you close the sale; it's when you ask the brand-new customer for referrals. Asking for referrals from customers, prospects, and others, when done right, can help you build a significant amount of business from such leads. Because referrals are much easier to close than cold leads, one referral can replace a number of cold calls. Once you've gotten a referral from a particular source, you'll need to handle both the referral and the referral source correctly to maximize the amount of business you get. Treating the referral well means the person who referred him will be likely to continue referring leads to you. You can greatly expand your referral base by sending out referral request emails and letters; by drafting a handful of templates, you can quickly produce the perfect letter for any potential referral source. As your experience with referrals grows, you may wish to take the step of creating your own referral group. Such a group can provide you with a regular flow of highly qualified leads. Finally, if you want to boost your referrals to the point where you're getting a significant percentage of your sales from them, you'll need to develop a referral network that goes well beyond a local group.

THE IMPORTANCE OF REFERRALS

Leads for Free

Referrals—otherwise known as getting someone to give you warm leads for free—are valuable for salespeople in all industries. Yet it's amazing how few salespeople really work at getting significant numbers of referrals.

Studies show that the typical salesperson is six times more likely to make a sale to a referral than she is to make a sale to an ordinary cold lead. That means you can potentially get six times as many sales if you emphasize finding referrals than you would if you spent the same amount of time cold calling. And once you start really looking for them, you'll see endless opportunities for referrals from the people around you.

NEW CUSTOMERS

Referrals are the last stage of the sales cycle for good reason. Just after you've closed someone is the best time to get referrals from him, because he's excited about his new purchase. It's common for salespeople to be nervous about asking for referrals right after closing; in that moment of limp relief after having managed to land a sale, all you want to do is get out of there and collapse.

However, asking for a referral at this point is not in the least scary or confrontational. Your new customer is probably thrilled and enthusiastic about having just made a purchase that's going to improve his life. Giving you a referral means creating an opportunity for a friend or colleague to have the same thrill he's feeling now. Hit him up for a referral while his excitement is at its peak, and you're much more likely to get a few good referrals than you would be a week from now.

EXISTING CUSTOMERS

Your current customers are usually the easiest and most cooperative referral sources. In fact, if you treat them right, they may well become advocates for you and bring you new leads without your even asking. That's where those wonderful windfall calls come from, when you pick up the phone and hear someone's coworker or brother saying, "I've heard you sell the best [fill in your product] in town. I'd like to buy thirty."

Customer Loyalty

Would you be surprised to hear that asking your customers for referrals makes them more loyal? Recommending other people to you locks in your customers as your advocates; psychologically, they're committed to you and are less likely to switch to another provider.

Better still, don't wait for your customers to think of this on their own—start calling around and ask them for referrals. It's a good idea anyway to speak with new customers a few weeks and/or months after the sale. You can find out if they're enjoying the product, ask if they have any questions, and then hit them with your request: "Who else do you know who would benefit from owning this product, just as you have?"

PROSPECTS WHO DIDN'T BUY

If you get an appointment with a prospect and she decides not to buy, don't just leave quietly with your head hanging. Get a referral or two, and you'll be able to walk out of there with something of value.

It may sound crazy to ask for referrals from someone who wouldn't even buy from you, but it's actually a great opportunity. A lot of sales fall through not because the prospect doesn't like your product, but because the product just isn't what she's looking for. In that case the prospect may well know someone who *is* a good fit.

Also, most people don't like saying no to someone else's request—it makes them uncomfortable. If they turn down the purchase and then you ask for a referral, prospects will often unconsciously see this as a chance to make it up to you and will make a real effort to come up with good leads for you.

EVERYONE YOU'VE EVER MET

Literally anyone you know or meet under any circumstances can give you a referral. The average person knows more than 250 other people. Among those hundreds of people, some are bound to be a good fit for your products. All you have to do is explain briefly what your product does, and then ask who the person knows who could use said product. Ask everyone—your dry-cleaner, the guy who does your taxes, your next-door neighbor, even the person standing in line behind you in the supermarket. Once you get in the habit of asking, you'll be amazed how many great leads you can collect just from having a short conversation.

AFTER YOU GET A REFERRAL

How to Make the Most of Everyone

The first time you get a referral from someone, you'll learn a few important details about the referrer. First, you now know that he's convinced enough about the value of your product to give you referrals. After all, if he refers someone to you and that person has a disappointing experience with the product, it could ruin the referred person's opinion of him—so most people won't make referrals unless they're fairly sure that the product is a good one.

Second, you know he has a good opinion of *you*. He's trusting you not to rip off the person he's referring or otherwise give the person a bad experience.

Finally, you'll discover how well the referrer understands you and your products. If the person he refers to you is someone who isn't really a prospect, then the referrer doesn't understand what you're looking for. That means you need to put a little more time into explaining what your product does, how it works, and who can benefit from it.

LEARNING FROM A REFERRAL

These bits of information that you learn from someone's first referral are at least as valuable as the referral itself, because it will help you to generate more referrals from that referrer. His referrals will only improve as time goes on, if you know how to treat him right.

If the person he refers is someone relatively unimportant to him, it implies that he doesn't trust you all that much. By giving you someone's name, he's all but promising that person that you and your product can add value for him. If you then let the referred person down in some way, that person's opinion of the referrer may take a turn for the worse. That's why referrers generally won't refer people whose opinions they value unless they trust you quite well. Putting in an effort to build rapport with your referrer can result in more and better referrals down the road.

On the other hand, if the referral is way off base, then you need to educate the referrer a bit better. He clearly wants to help by providing referrals to you; he just doesn't understand exactly what you need. He also doesn't want to sit there for a long time and listen to you talk about your products and your business. So you'll need to find a way to be brief and yet explicit when you explain the kind of referrals you're looking for. One possible approach is to type up a simple letter with the same qualities and factors that you look for when you qualify prospects and give it to your referrers.

Always remember that your referrers aren't giving you referrals just to be helpful (although most people enjoy that aspect of it); they refer people to you because they want to be heroes to those people. Most referrers will happily give you as many referrals as they can if they are convinced you'll do an excellent job for them, because they get gratitude and perhaps also a stronger relationship with each person they refer. Your referrers will feel much better about giving you more referrals if you show how much you appreciate that. Appreciation doesn't have to come in an expensive or significant form either; something as simple as a thank-you note or an e-card can be plenty for a typical referral. If a referrer does something above and beyond the usual, such as sending you someone who makes an enormous purchase or aggressively recommending you to others, you can do something special for him in return: take him out to dinner, buy him a gift basket, or whatever you think he'll really enjoy.

RESPECT THE REFERRAL

How you handle your first referral from someone will likely determine whether you get more referrals from that person. In fact, if you mistreat someone who's been referred to you, then that referrer may start doing negative referrals—he'll tell everyone he knows how awful you are. That's why it's crucial to provide exceptional service to anyone who gets referred to you, especially the first referral someone sends you. This doesn't mean giving him a huge discount or going to ridiculous lengths to please him, but it does mean finding ways to meet that person's needs and prioritizing those needs. For example, if the referral needs a particular model of your product that's not currently available, you might reach out to your contacts in the warehouse to get him the very next one that's available. Or you might personally deliver the product to him and help him set it up. Once you've proven that you can and will do a great job for anyone that person refers to you, he'll be eager to send you more.

Other People's Mistakes

What if the mistake isn't yours but is the fault of someone else in your company? Assume the blame anyway. People don't want to hear excuses; they want their problems solved. If something goes wrong, apologize, tell them how you're going to fix it, and then fix it.

It's especially important to resolve any mistakes you make in a fast and professional manner, and also tell the referrer what went wrong and how you fixed it. If you make a mistake but then do an excellent job of handling the situation, you may actually end up impressing the person more than if you'd never made a mistake.

It's a good idea to keep in touch with the referrer during the sales process. You don't need to inform him of every little thing that happens; just touch base occasionally to let him know how it's going. You might even turn to the referrer as a resource, although it's a bad idea to abuse this privilege. For example, if you're having a hard time convincing the referral to move on through the sales process, you might ask the referrer for a few tips about how that person thinks. This advice can help you figure out what's delaying the sales process and what you can do to move things along.

Finally, remember to thank the referrer whether or not you close a sale with the person he referred. He's done you a big favor just by sending someone to you, so show him that you understand that.

WRITING REFERRAL REQUEST LETTERS

Ask and You Shall Receive

Referral request letters can help you make widespread requests for referrals in the most efficient manner. Once you have a few referral request templates, you can easily customize your letters and send them out either by email or by snail mail.

Mail or Email?

Email is the cheapest and most efficient way to send out referral request letters. However, sending such a letter by postal mail will help you to get the recipient's attention. Just be sure to prepare your letter and envelope in such a way that it's obviously not junk mail.

You can create different templates to use for different audiences in your quest for referrals. Here are a few examples to get you started.

FOR CURRENT CUSTOMERS

Your existing customers can be a great source of referrals. Sending them a referral request letter once a year or so will keep you top-of-mind as well as give you a chance to refresh your customers on what you're looking for in a referral.

Dear [customer name],

I hope you're continuing to enjoy success with [product or service], like [mention a particular success they've had using your product]. I'd like to spread those benefits out to some of your friends and colleagues who have needs similar to your own.

Would you consider providing the names and contact information of people you know who would benefit from [product or service]?

Here are a few examples of the benefits my [product/service/products and services] can provide:

- [Benefit 1]
- [Benefit 2]
- [Benefit 3]
- [Benefit 4]

I work with many types of [customers/clients], but the [customers/clients] who tend to benefit the most from this [product or service] include those with:

- [Customer attribute]
- [Customer attribute]
- [Customer attribute]

If you know someone—or several people—who share these qualities, please reply with their names and contact information. I may mention your name when I get in touch with them; please let me know if that's all right with you.

Thanks again for your business! Please feel free to reach out if you have any questions about how to get the most out of your [product or service], and I'll be happy to assist.

Sincerely,
[your name]

FOR MEMBERS OF YOUR NETWORK, ESPECIALLY OTHER SALESPEOPLE

Network contacts can be quite helpful at providing referrals, as can salespeople at other companies (assuming they're not your competitors). As you'll learn in the next section, referral groups allow you to exchange leads with other salespeople, generally resulting in increased sales for both parties. This template is a good way to get a referral group started or to add new members to an existing group.

Dear [name],

I hope this email finds you well. I wanted to take the opportunity to reconnect with you and also let you know what I'm up to these days. I am now working as a [your job title] for [your company]. Since you're in a similar line of work, I thought I'd check if you would like to be part of my referral team. The primary objective of this team is to support each other and share referrals and other opportunities to build our businesses.

Each member becomes a resource for everyone else in the group, not only for providing new leads but also as a resource for all our clients who might need our services.

Here are a few examples of the benefits that my [product/service/products and services] can provide:

- [Benefit 1]
- [Benefit 2]
- [Benefit 3]
- [Benefit 4]

I work with many types of [customers/clients], but my ideal [customer/client] has the following qualities:

- [Customer attribute]
- [Customer attribute]
- [Customer attribute]

If my ideal [customer/client] type sounds familiar, I'd love to talk with you so that I can learn more about what you need for your business and how you would want me to send you the referrals I generate for you. And if you know anyone who is interested in some or all of the benefits I mentioned, I would be happy to chat with them to see if my [product/service] is a good fit.

Feel free to contact me any time at [your phone number] or email me at [your email address]. Thanks again for your time, and I look forward to speaking with you soon.

Regards,
[your name]

You can easily customize these templates to work for any number of recipients. For example, if you want a referral letter to send to a prospect who didn't buy from you, you can change the first paragraph of the customer template letter and you'll have exactly what you need. Over time, as you see how people respond to your letters and emails, you'll be able to tweak your templates to get the best possible results.

REFERRAL GROUPS

The Referral Buddy System

Since all salespeople share the need for leads, you can easily set up a referral group that includes you and other local salespeople. Obviously, you wouldn't recruit salespeople working for your competitors, but salespeople in every other industry are fair game.

Ideally, you'll be able to bring in a number of salespeople from related industries whose preferred customers overlap with your own. For example, let's say you sell athletic shoes. If you have a referral partner who sells gym memberships at a nearby gym, then your prospects will almost certainly be a good fit for her and vice versa. But salespeople in completely unrelated industries can often provide a number of useful leads, so don't leave them out of your group.

You can also cast your net a bit wider and invite people who aren't in sales to join your group. For example, professionals such as lawyers, accountants, and doctors can be terrific sources of referrals, and you can repay them with referrals of your own.

Before you invite someone to join your referral group, make sure it's someone you wouldn't be ashamed to recommend, with a decent-quality product or service. When you suggest a particular person or product to a customer and she acts on your recommendation, she is doing so based on her trust in you. If the recommended product turns out to be a poor-quality item, the customer will be less inclined to trust you in the future. In a worst-case scenario you might even lose that customer. For that reason, stick with group members whom you can be proud to recommend.

Keep in mind that your customers may not be thrilled with you if you're constantly giving their contact information to other salespeople. You'll need to walk a fine line between sharing enough referrals with other members of the group so that they don't think you're a freeloader, and not driving your customers crazy. Generally speaking, if you refer your customers only to people you genuinely believe can be of benefit to them, you'll be fine.

You'll have to decide how the new referral group will operate. Some groups like to meet every other week or so over coffee or lunch and exchange leads, others pass along referrals as they become available, and some groups do both.

If you choose the regular meeting option, you might want to set a minimum requirement for group members so no one's time is wasted. For example, you might make a rule that each member must bring at least six good-quality referrals for one or more other members of the group, and anyone who doesn't have enough referrals has to pay for lunch. If a particular person is constantly short on referrals, that's a sign that he may not belong in your group.

During each lunch meeting a particular member of the group might make a brief presentation about his product and what he looks for in a customer, so the other members of the group know what kind of people to refer to him. This is a great opportunity for group members to refine their elevator speeches.

The Elevator Speech

An elevator speech is a brief but compelling message about what's great about you, your company, and/or your product. An elevator speech should take no more than thirty seconds to deliver and should inspire the listener to ask for more information.

You'll also need to decide how aggressive group members will be in promoting referrals. Will they pass on a name and phone number to another group member, or will they actively recommend group members to their customers?

As your referral group grows, you may find it helpful to put together a brief directory of its members. Each member can contribute a paragraph or two about their product or service, and you can hand out the pamphlets to anyone you think would benefit from knowing one or more members of the group.

It's a good idea to include a mix of seasoned professionals and relatively new salespeople in your referral group. The experienced salespeople will tend to have a larger pool of potential leads to pass out to other group members, while the newcomers will likely have a lot more energy and "hustle." Combining both types of salespeople in one group will make for a good flow of referrals for everybody. The newbies will have the chance to learn some new tricks and tactics from the group's more experienced members, while the pros will benefit from an ever-growing flow of referrals as the newbies master their sales skills.

BUILDING A HEALTHY REFERRAL CYCLE

Going Beyond Referral Groups

How would you like to have an ongoing flow of good referrals coming in? It's possible, but you won't accomplish it just by hitting up new customers at the end of the sales cycle (although that's a great place to start). A strong, self-supporting referral cycle not only provides you with hot leads; it also means you have less need for cold calling to keep your sales pipeline filled. More leads with less cold calling is definitely an ideal situation for salespeople!

Customers and prospects are a great place to start looking for referrals. However, most customers won't be able to send you very many referrals, certainly not enough to fill your pipeline or replace significant amounts of cold calling. If you're lucky, a good customer might send you two or three quality referrals a year, along with a handful of other referrals that don't actually qualify as prospects.

Competing Referral Sources

As you build up your referral sources, you'll inevitably end up working with salespeople from different companies in the same industry, so you'll need a system to determine which salesperson gets which referral. You might rotate among them on a regular schedule, or direct referrals to whoever's the best fit.

The best source of ongoing referrals is other salespeople. If you've already started or joined a referral group, you've taken a good step toward building a significant amount of new business from referrals. However, a referral group is only a starting place. For example, there will likely be many salespeople who don't want to commit to a group but will be willing to exchange referrals on a less formal, one-on-one basis. If you already have a referral group member who belongs to a certain industry, he may not be willing to have other members of the group who are his direct competitors. If you want referral relationships with these competitors, you'll need to set them up separately.

As with a referral group, motivating your fellow salespeople to help you with referrals is simple: you commit to sending them referrals right back. Turning your relationship into a referral collaboration will make your fellow salespeople not only willing but also eager to send you more and more referrals.

The first step in setting up one-on-one referral collaborations is identifying the salespeople who are great sources of qualified referrals, and are also people to whom you can send good-quality referrals. For example, if you're selling mortgage loans, your local realtors would be an ideal source for referrals. The realtors can send you prospects who are shopping for houses but who haven't yet secured financing, and you can send them prospects who've gotten mortgage prequalifications before connecting with a realtor on their own.

Next, decide exactly what kind of arrangement you want to propose to your potential referral sources. Do you want to just swap referrals back and forth, or do you want to arrange a more active partnership? For example, an active partnership with your referral collaborators could include setting up joint sales campaigns, going on sales calls together, or hosting an event for both your prospects or customers. It's best to start off small—once you get to know your referral partners better, you'll have a better idea of which ones you want to work with more closely.

GETTING IN TOUCH WITH
POTENTIAL REFERRALS

Now you're ready to get in touch with your potential referral sources. You should approach this conversation just as you would a sales pitch to a major prospect. In other words, don't randomly call up a potential referral collaborator and ask her to send you referrals. Instead, schedule a meeting with her and come prepared to persuade. A lunch meeting often works well—in which case you'd offer to pay for lunch.

When you call to set up the meeting, you can simply say that you're familiar with her reputation as one of the top sellers in her industry, and you'd like to get to know her a little better because you like to be on good terms with the best people in your area. This is usually persuasive enough to get your potential referral source to agree to a meeting.

When you're face-to-face and have finished exchanging pleasantries, it's time to present your proposal. Again, you need to approach this as you would a sales presentation—in this case you're pitching yourself as a valuable resource to your fellow salesperson. Testimonials from mutual customers or existing referral sources can be a great way to demonstrate your value. Even better, come with a couple of referrals to give her on the spot so that you can prove your value to your potential collaborator.

Once your new referral source agrees to the relationship, be sure to send her at least as many referrals as she sends you—if not more. As the proposer of this arrangement, you've got to give her plenty of reason to value your association. If all goes well during the first few months, you'll have established yourself in her mind as a valued resource and will be able to draw on her for referrals indefinitely. Multiply that by a few dozen similar referral sources, and you may be able to give up cold calling altogether.

CHAPTER 8

COLD CALLING—WITH OR WITHOUT A PHONE

Unless you're lucky enough to have someone else in the office taking care of the cold calling, you'll likely have to do at least some cold calling to get enough prospects. Most people really don't enjoy cold calling, but it's still the most effective way to get leads into your pipeline. You'll likely have a mix of both cold leads and warm leads to work with; it's important to know the right way to handle each type of lead. Many prospects will require several calls before you can reach them, let alone get them to schedule an appointment; a well-planned cold calling sequence can help maximize the number of appointments you get from such prospects. Certain common mistakes can make your cold calling far less effective, so you'll need to watch out for them. While most people think of cold calling as synonymous with making phone calls, in reality cold calling encompasses a number of different sales channels. When you make cold calls, you'll be competing with other salespeople in the same industry, so you'll need to know how to prevail. Finally, a strong cold call opener and closer are a crucial part of sales success.

COLD CALLS VERSUS WARM CALLS

How to Handle Each Type

Cold calling is connecting with a brand-new lead, while warm calling refers to calling a prospect with whom you've had some prior contact. The warmer a lead is, the easier it will typically be to close a sale with him. Few leads are totally cold or totally warm; they tend to fall somewhere along the spectrum between those two points.

For example, your company's marketing department will generally send lists of businesses or individuals who have expressed some interest in your products to the various sales teams. At the very least, these leads are one step better than cold call leads because you know that they're members of a relevant industry (for B2B leads) or demographic group (for B2C leads). Just how warm these leads are will depend on how marketing collected them for you.

Finding Your Own Warm Leads

If you don't have a marketing department sending you warm leads—or if you feel that you can use more leads than you get from them—you might consider sourcing your own warm leads. The easiest way to do so is by soliciting referrals, a subject that's addressed in Chapter 7.

If you don't already know what approach the marketing team used to get those leads, ask them. Knowing where the contact information came from can help you to figure out the best way to open a conversation with those leads.

The "coldest" of warm leads are the ones who have been purchased from a lead list provider or other source. Usually the leads on these lists have signed up to receive a newsletter or freemium from a company similar to your own, and have agreed to release their information to affiliates. Your employer is one of those affiliates. What makes these leads slightly warmer is that they've expressed interest in hearing from companies related to the one they requested the download or newsletter from. However, they may not be thrilled to hear from your particular company—in fact, many people who sign up for freemiums and have agreed to speak to affiliates forget that they've given their consent, and assume that you're just cold calling them.

Next up are leads that have signed up to receive information specifically from your company. They may not be interested in buying something right away, but they are interested enough in your company and its products to have downloaded a document or signed up for a special offer. Such leads have heard of your company, have some faith in its reputation, and are at least mildly interested in hearing more. That puts them several steps above cold leads with regard to how hard you'll have to work to get an appointment and/or close a sale with them.

Some companies allow potential customers to sign up for a free trial of their services. If your company provides that option, then the leads that come from these free trial offers are valuable indeed. These are people who are interested in your product, may have already started using it, and hopefully like what they see. In fact, if your free trial leads have already started using the product as a replacement for whatever they were using before, then for once you'll have prospect inertia working in your favor. It's much simpler for these prospects to just buy your product and keep on using it than it is for them to start searching all over again for the right product for their needs.

Finally, the warmest of all leads are the ones who have requested a call from a salesperson. These leads represent prospects who are just about ready to buy, and while there are no sure things in sales, they are about as close as you can get to one.

A common mistake salespeople make with warm leads is to assume that because it's not a cold call, they can take the sale for granted. But just because it's a nice warm lead, that doesn't mean that you can skip over entire stages of the sales process. A lead is still not a customer or even a prospect. In order to take full advantage of those warm leads, you need to approach them with the same respect as you would a cold lead.

Warm lead or not, your first conversation should focus on establishing the value your product can offer and getting the prospect interested. You will also need to qualify the lead to confirm that he is indeed a prospect, no matter how hot a lead he seems to be. You can't assume that a lead is a prospect even if he has asked to speak with a salesperson, because he may not know whether the product is a good fit. In fact, that may well be why he wants to talk to you—so that he can get more information from someone who's an expert in the product and confirm whether it's the best option.

Finally, it's important to respond to warm leads as quickly as possible. If you let a few days go by before picking up the phone, the person may have forgotten all about asking for more information and you'll have to start from scratch as a cold call. On the other hand, a quick response can reassure the lead that you will provide excellent service in the future, which will help incline him toward buying from you.

SCHEDULING YOUR COLD CALL SEQUENCE

Plan and Execute

Decision-makers tend to be very busy people. If you're selling to other businesses, you're reaching out to executives and purchasing department employees who probably field dozens or even hundreds of phone calls and emails every day. If you're selling to individuals, you're calling people who (just like you) are juggling their work and home duties. As a result, most salespeople have to make several phone calls just to reach a decision-maker, let alone convince her to schedule an appointment. Regular cold callers leave lots and lots of voicemail messages, and keeping track of all those messages and return calls requires a planned cold call sequence.

First, you'll need to figure out how many calls is too many and what's a reasonable time frame for reaching out to a decision-maker after having already called or emailed him. Salespeople who give up after one or two contact attempts are throwing away a whole lot of sales. On the other hand, calling a decision-maker every day for a month is going to make the prospect feel like you're stalking her, not convince her to buy something from you.

The best cold calling sequence for you will depend on your sales strategy and the type of product you sell. Start by planning out a sequence for contacting leads once a week over a period of four weeks. If you sell an expensive, low-volume product and/or sell to CEOs and other high-level executives, you might run your sequence as long as eight weeks with eight separate contact attempts.

Each time you leave a message, refer to the last message you left (or email you sent) and let her know when your next contact attempt will come. Don't forget to leave your contact information and a time or two when you'll be available, so that the prospect can reach out to you before then if she's ready to move forward.

If you've already made several contact attempts without reaching a human being, try calling at a different time or on a different day of the week. Busy executives are most often available for phone calls very early in the morning, before their assistants arrive and while the executive is answering the phone herself. Consumers are often available early in the evening (but not during dinnertime!) and on weekends. However, if you've been trying to reach an executive early in the morning and never get her, try calling late in the day—perhaps she's a night owl and prefers to work evenings rather than mornings.

Don't forget that cold calling isn't limited to just phone calls. Decision-makers who are all but impossible to reach by phone may be easily available by email. Snail mail can also be an effective way to reach certain prospects, especially if you have some interesting item or fact to share, such as a magazine article about the prospect or a brand-new piece of news that's relevant to her industry.

Alternating Contact Methods

Using a sequence of different contact methods, such as phone, email, and social media, can be more effective than making endless phone calls. Just make sure that you count each attempted contact as one step in your sequence, so you're not bombarding decision-makers with messages.

Dropping by the prospect's office in person can be a good way to get ahold of the more elusive prospects and show how serious you are about talking to them. If you use one of these non-phone channels to reach a prospect, count it as your contact attempt for the week and then mention it in the next phone call you make to him. For example, you might say, "I hope you got that newspaper clipping I sent you last Monday—congratulations on that acquisition!").

If you're getting held up by a gatekeeper rather than by the prospect's voicemail system, then your only chance at reaching the prospect is to turn the gatekeeper into a coconspirator. Each time you speak with her, write down a few notes about the conversation—particularly the gatekeeper's name. Then the next time you call, you can bring up or comment about one of the things you wrote down to show the gatekeeper that you're paying attention to what she has to say. It's amazing how much a spouse or administrative assistant will appreciate a simple courtesy like really listening to and thinking about what she has to say. If you can get the gatekeeper on your side, reaching the decision-maker will be easy. For that matter, if you convince the gatekeeper that speaking with you will be worthwhile, she might even add you to the decision-maker's calendar! And since gatekeepers often act as advisers, you're more likely to close the sale if she's recommending you to the decision-maker.

If you've completed your planned cold calling sequence and still haven't managed to schedule an appointment, set aside that lead for now. You can reach out to him again three to six months from now and see if he is more willing to consider a purchase. As long as there's still a chance that the lead might be a prospect and might buy from you, don't give up on him.

COMMON COLD CALLING MISTAKES

Sound Familiar?

Cold calling is controversial among salespeople these days. Some salespeople have great success with it, yet others insist that "cold calling is dead" and connecting with warm leads is the only way to sell. If you, too, have struggled with cold calling, it could be because you're making one of the following common mistakes.

SELLING DURING THE COLD CALL

Cold calls aren't the right venue for selling your product or service. During the cold call you're talking to someone you've never met or spoken with before today—it's unlikely that she'll be willing to buy something from a total stranger. Would you?

When Prospects Ask about Features

Some prospects will insist on learning about the product's features before they'll meet with you. Go ahead and answer one or two questions, but if the prospect wants a lot of detail, say that it would be better to go into more depth in person.

Instead of selling your product during cold calls, focus on selling the appointment. Tantalize your prospect with hints of what she'll learn during the appointment, and if she asks for specific product information, do your best to hold her off until you can meet with her in person.

NOT OFFERING VALUE

The intent behind cold calling leads is to get them just interested enough to be willing to schedule an appointment with you (and actually show up). To do that, you need to motivate them by showing them they have something to gain from meeting with you. This could be a specific gift, such as a freemium, or a more general offer of value. For example, you could point out that by meeting with you the prospect will learn useful information about this type of product that will turn him into a smarter shopper and help ensure that he picks out just the right one for his needs.

NOT DOING ENOUGH COLD CALLING

Finally, we come to the most serious and most common mistake of all: not devoting enough time or energy to cold calling prospects. Salespeople of all experience levels and walks of life find a remarkable range of reasons not to cold call. Consider if any of the following rationalizations sound familiar.

The Reluctant Salesperson
Many salespeople sort of fall into sales when they can't get jobs in their preferred career paths, and many of them are a bit embarrassed by the job. When asked what they do for a living, they tend to use titles

like "account manager" or other less-obvious names for their sales jobs. Because they're ashamed of what they do, they tend to think that anyone they cold call will be disgusted. So reluctant salespeople avoid cold calling as much as they can, and when they're forced to make calls, they're very apologetic about it. Reluctant salespeople need to realize that they have nothing to be embarrassed about. A salesperson's job is really to identify people who have a certain problem, and then connect those people with the product that solves that problem. It's a win-win-win calling: the new customer gets his needs met, the company that makes the product gets its revenue, and the salesperson pockets a commission.

The Fearful Salesperson

Sooner or later all cold callers will run into a really unpleasant person who will react explosively to being called. Salespeople making cold calls get cursed at, hung up on, and abused—from time to time. The fearful salesperson has a very hard time recovering from the most unpleasant calls. He may be a new salesperson or a very sensitive person, or he may have low self-esteem. For whatever reason, because he dreads the rare confrontational call, he avoids cold calls as much as possible. When he does make calls, he is very timid in what he says and does. Fearful salespeople need to find a way to feel more comfortable about being rejected during cold calls and other sales situations. Growing a thicker skin just takes practice and a slight change to the mindset.

The Perfectionist Salesperson

Doing pre-call research makes cold calling far more effective, but some salespeople take this to extremes. The perfectionist salesperson feels that the more she knows about a prospect in advance, the better she will be able to sell to him—which is true. However, these salespeople may spend an hour or more researching every single prospect they intend to call. In rare cases an extremely valuable prospect might be worth this level of attention, but putting tons of time into researching every single prospect means you'll never have the time to actually sell to these people. Perfectionist salespeople need to realize and accept that they can't take the time to learn every little detail about every prospect. They can improve their cold calling results by putting themselves on a timer that allows them only a certain number of minutes of research per prospect.

The Superstar Salesperson

Success can be a much bigger problem than failure, if the successful person doesn't handle it well. Some salespeople who've experienced the thrill of landing a major sale become addicted to the heady feeling and want to spend all their time working on closing sales. Sitting at a desk making cold call after cold call has no appeal compared with scoring another huge sale and becoming the office hero. There's just one tiny problem: without those tedious cold calls, you won't have the prospects you need to score another big win. Superstars have to realize that cold calling is a necessary part of the job and a prerequisite to its more thrilling aspects.

ALTERNATIVE COLD CALLING METHODS

Phone Calls Aren't the Only Option

While the majority of cold calling is done over the phone, alternatives do exist. The most common alternative to phone cold calling is email cold calling. While you can use just email to reach leads, using it in combination with the phone is typically the most effective approach, since they complement each other. Using both contact methods can supercharge your prospecting efforts, but only if you synchronize them correctly.

Early on in the sales process you can alternate between phone calls and email as a way to strengthen your message. For example, you might start by phoning the prospect, and as soon as you hang up with her, send an email summarizing what you discussed on the phone and confirming the appointment you just set with her. This way, you're giving a prospect two different ways to reach you, plus a reminder—in writing—of when you'll be meeting with her. Better yet, attach a calendar file to the email so that the prospect can click on the attachment and automatically add your appointment to her calendar.

Some prospects have a strong preference for email, while others only respond well to phone calls. By using both methods, you can quickly figure out which approach gets faster responses from a particular prospect. You can then use that contact method every time you reach out to the prospect.

Using email does have one potential drawback: people will expect an email response about twice as quickly as they would expect a call back after leaving a voicemail. If you receive an email with a prospect's question and you simply don't have an answer for her, or you're busy and can't respond in full right away, send a brief email reply acknowledging her message and saying that you'll get back to her with an answer as soon as possible.

Remember that your emails, unlike phone conversations, are in writing and are relatively permanent. Read through every email at least once before you click Send, checking it over for spelling errors and other problems. If anything you wrote seems unclear or potentially controversial, rephrase it. Also, emails should usually be brief and to the point. If you have a long or complicated explanation to make, give a brief overview in your email and explain that you're going to give the person a call so that you can go into it in more detail over the phone. Or offer to set up a meeting in which you can go over the subject in person.

What about Social Media?

Social media is a great tool for responding to *warm* leads, positioning yourself as an expert, and business networking. However, it's not a great choice for cold calling. People tend to get annoyed with social media solicitations and consider them spam.

It can be very tempting to shift the bulk of your cold calling over to email, especially for salespeople who really hate cold calling over the phone. However, if you're not combining phone with email, you'll be subject to email's weaknesses as a sales channel—namely, that it's easy to ignore; prospects might glance over your subject line and hit Delete without ever reading your messages.

Before voicemail and email became part of everyday life, many salespeople preferred to physically visit prospects instead of calling them on the phone. It's not as common an approach today, especially in B2B sales, which means that it can be quite useful and effective. After all, if you're the first salesperson who has stopped by a particular office, novelty can help you get your foot in the door.

When you cold call in person, you should give the prospect a plausible reason for your being there. For example, if you have an appointment nearby, you can say something like, "I was just speaking with the family next door and I have a few minutes to spare, so I'd be happy to do a fifteen-minute security assessment for you at no charge," or whatever type of offer suits the products and services you sell. Another option is to say, "I've just started working in this part of town, and I wanted to say hello and get to know the people in this neighborhood."

In-person cold calling works best if you keep your visits extremely low pressure—people don't react well when someone bursts into their home or office and starts pitching them. Your goal is to get the name and phone number of the decision-maker (you can do this by exchanging business cards in a B2B scenario) and perhaps do a bit of prequalifying. You can then follow up with a phone call or email to schedule an appointment with the prospect.

Finally, direct mail is another traditional way to reach leads, but it is also the most expensive. A basic letter (assuming you write it yourself) will cost you only the envelope, paper, and stamps, but if you hire a designer to put together a professional direct mail package, you can end up spending a great deal of money. On the other hand, if you have a good lead list and a skilled designer, such a package can have an impressive response rate.

COPING WITH COMPETITORS

Protecting Your Precious Prospects

Most prospects will do some comparison shopping before they make the decision to buy. The more expensive a product or service is, the more research and comparing prospects will do. After all, if a lot of money is on the line, they want to make sure they're getting the best possible product with the best possible value.

When you first engage a prospect, you won't know where he is in the buying process. If he's fairly early in the process—perhaps he hadn't even thought of buying your type of product or service before you spoke with him—you have a big advantage over the competition. You'll be able to help the prospect figure out his buying criteria, with an emphasis on the ones that will favor your company. For example, if your product is an industry leader in reliability, you can point out to the prospect how a reliable product can save him money over the long term and will be much more convenient because it won't be continually breaking down. In these cases winning in the prospect's comparison-shopping research is fairly easy given your head start.

Unique Selling Propositions

A unique selling proposition is a specific factor that makes a particular product different from and better than the competition. Your marketing department probably already has one or two of these; you can also come up with your own.

If the prospect is farther along in the buying process when you cold call him, one or more of your competitors has probably already spoken to him. That means you've lost the opportunity to rig the prospect's buying criteria in your favor.

In this situation the smart move is to try to reframe those buying criteria in order to come out a little better when the prospect ranks you and your competitors. This is a great time to bring up your unique selling proposition (USP). Since your USP is, by definition, unique, you'll be the only one able to provide it.

If you can't budge the prospect's buying criteria at this point, your next best option is to find a way to add value. For example, you might offer the prospect an extended free trial, add in an upgrade at no charge, or include a long-term maintenance package at a reduced price. The idea is to win points for your product against your competitors as the prospect's comparison shopping continues.

If you have the feeling that you're not the prospect's first choice, try slowing down his buying process. That probably sounds strange, given that salespeople are always trying to get prospects moving faster toward the close, but it's an effective tactic in this situation.

First, it'll give you more time to work on the prospect and hopefully convince him that your product is the superior choice. And second, slowing down the prospect's buying process may cause whichever competitor is currently winning the race to panic and ruin his own chances.

You can usually slow down the buying process just by pointing out potential issues or concerns that the prospect may not have considered. Another useful approach is to bring up something that will happen in the near future that might affect which product is the prospect's best choice. For example, you might mention that your company is releasing a new model of your product in six months, and the new model will be an excellent fit for the prospect's needs.

If all else fails, you can still try to acquire a small piece of business from the prospect even if you can't sell him the big-ticket item that he's decided to buy from a competitor. Convincing the prospect to buy even a tiny product or service gives you a foot in the door that may lead to much larger sales in the future. You've probably already noticed that it's much easier to sell to an existing customer than to a new prospect, so converting a prospect to a customer (even in a very small way) is a victory.

Depending on the nature of your product or service and the prospect's current situation, you might either try to sell him one part of the package that you were originally trying to convince him to buy, or you can pitch him an unreated small product. If the prospect just wasn't willing to buy your major product or package, he'll probably be quite a bit more open to buying a less expensive product or service—assuming that you can show him there's value in acquiring the small product.

Even if the sale falls apart completely and you lose the chance to sell anything, keep the door open for future sales by behaving in a pleasant and businesslike manner (which includes not bad-mouthing your competitors, no matter how strongly you're tempted). After all, it's possible that the competitor who's about to win the prospect's business will bungle things in some way and you'll suddenly end up as the new front-runner. Or the prospect might call you a few months from now because the product he bought from a competitor just isn't working as well as he hoped. Imagine how sweet it would feel to snatch away the sale from your competitor at the last moment just because you acted like a professional and he didn't.

COLD CALL OPENERS AND CLOSERS

The High Note

The first fifteen seconds of your cold call will most likely determine whether or not you get an appointment with that prospect. That's the time during which the person you're calling realizes that you're a salesperson, which causes most people to go into auto-rejection mode and stop listening to you. If you can say something during those first fifteen seconds that grabs her attention, you can surprise her into listening to you instead of just saying no thanks and hanging up.

As you learned in Chapter 3, cold call openers often include a question. That's because questions by their very nature are more likely to get the listener thinking than are statements. If you can, also work the lead's name into the question—or at least somewhere into your opener. People tend to pay more attention when they hear their own names.

Here's an example of a cold call opener that incorporates both a surprising bit of information and a question. This example is taken from a real estate broker's script, but it's general enough to apply to almost any product or service.

Lead: "Hello?"
You: "Would you like to save an additional ten thousand dollars this year?"
Lead: "Who is this?"

You: "My name is [your name], and I show people how to save an additional ten thousand dollars; would you like to learn how to do it?"

Lead: "What's this about?"

You: "It's about saving an additional ten thousand dollars this year; would you like to learn more about it?"

Lead: "Is this some sort of scam?"

You: "No, I can show you how to save an additional ten thousand dollars this year; it's what I specialize in. Would you like to learn more?"

Lead: "Who are you with?"

You: "I'm with [company name], and I specialize in saving my clients an additional..."

As you can see, the point of this opener is to keep emphasizing the benefit you offer and asking for permission to tell the lead more. Once the lead gives you that permission, you can then move into the rest of your cold call.

It's easy to develop your own cold call opener. Before you begin, you'll need three things:

- Who your prospective customers are
- How your product or service helps them
- A specific example of the benefits a customer has gotten

That last item is usually the trickiest, but if you poll your existing customers or check with your marketing department, you can likely find some outstanding examples of what your product is capable of. For example, let's say you sell janitorial services, and you find an example of a client who got his entire $6,000 security deposit back because your cleaning team managed to restore his offices to pristine condition. Your clients are typically small business owners, and your service helps them by keeping their offices perfectly clean at a reasonable price. In that case your custom cold call opener might sound like this: "My company helps small business owners like you maintain a client-ready office and has saved clients as much as six thousand dollars in a single visit."

Once you've got your cold call opener ready to go, it's time to focus on the second-most important part of the call: your closing statement. You've already learned that you have to close a sale yourself rather than hope the prospect does it for you. The same goes for cold calls, although what you're closing here is an appointment rather than a sale. Still, the principle is the same.

Turning Sales Closes Into Cold Call Closes

Since cold call closes operate on the same principle as sales closes, you can use the same methods for both. The only difference is that cold call closes need to highlight a benefit, since you won't have the chance during a cold call to talk up benefits in detail.

Your cold call closes will probably be similar in format to your sales closes. When you close a sale, you're asking the prospect to commit to giving you some of his money in exchange for whatever product or service you're selling. When you close a cold call, you're asking the prospect to commit to giving you some of his precious time so that you can spend it pitching a sale to him. For a cold call close to be successful, you need to show the prospect what he's getting out of that appointment in exchange for his time.

You can do this most blatantly by offering him a freemium, free trial, gift, or service that he will receive at the appointment. If you don't have anything like that to offer, you'll need to fall back on the product itself. During the body of the cold call, you'll share a few details about your product that will highlight its potential benefits; when you close, you'll touch on those benefits again briefly.

For example, let's say you've gotten the sense that the prospect is most interested in the convenience your janitorial service offers. When it's time to close the call, you might say something like, "I'd like to come over to your office and speak with you in person so that I can help you find a way to enjoy the convenience of our cleaning service at the best possible price. Is Monday at two p.m. a good time for you?" With such a close, you're pointing out what the prospect stands to gain and also "assuming the close" by asking a question that assumes the prospect will set an appointment.

CHAPTER 9
NETWORKING

If you don't already have a business network, today is a great day to get started. Networks take time to grow and start producing results, so don't expect instant gratification—but a few months or years from now, you'll be really glad you put in the time and energy now to start building your network. Networking is all about identifying people who may be useful in some way and creating reciprocal relationships with those people. While networking events such as Chamber of Commerce mixers and trade shows aren't as popular as they once were, they're still a highly useful tool for building and expanding on your network. Getting started is the toughest part of networking because you'll have to put in a fair amount of time and effort but you won't get results right away. As you build a good reputation for being a valuable network contact, growing and maintaining your network will become much easier. Many networkers consider social media to be the backbone of their business networks; it makes connecting with people all over the world not only possible but also painless. However, you'll need to plan your social media activities wisely to avoid frittering away your precious time.

BASIC BUSINESS NETWORKING

The Ground Rules

Just about every professional can gain enormous benefits from networking, but for salespeople these benefits are even greater. A strong business network can help you get more referrals; gain entrée to challenging prospects, such as *Fortune* 500 companies; find your dream job; acquire a mentor; and much more.

A lot of the skills you need to build and maintain a network are the same skills you already use to excel as a salesperson. So on top of networking's innate benefits, it's also a great opportunity to polish your sales skills.

Business networking isn't really complicated, but it does have some rules that a wise networker will follow. If you break these rules, you will lose a lot of your network contacts and could even damage your reputation with other potential contacts.

GIVE BEFORE YOU RECEIVE

If you begin your relationship with a new contact by asking for favors, you'll unquestionably give her the wrong impression. Networking is all about developing relationships. Consider what the effect on a friendship would be if you were continuously asking for favors without doing any in return.

Regretfully, a lot of networkers take exactly that approach. Therefore, it's vital to make it very clear that you aren't one of those people. The ideal way to do so is to provide at least a couple of favors for someone before you ask for something in return. They don't have to be big favors; it can be something as simple as giving the person a lead or forwarding an article on a topic that you know is relevant to him.

HAVE FUN WITH IT

A lot of professionals view business networking as a necessary evil, in much the same way that salespeople speak of cold calling. But if you approach people as though it's a chore, they aren't likely to be happy to hear from you. Instead, find a way to make your networking fun. You could turn it into a game, have a contest with others in your sales team to see who can pull off certain networking tasks, or integrate networking with doing something you've always wanted to do, like attending a networking event in a city you've always wanted to visit.

Volunteering is a wonderful way to network and do some good at the same time. You can volunteer for nonprofit organizations, churches, community outreach programs, or any other social program that seems particularly relevant to you. Volunteer positions usually require you to spend a significant amount of time helping out, but they will also give you the chance to meet people you might otherwise not be able to reach, and provide an excellent way to build rapport with those people.

KEEP SOCIAL NETWORKING SOCIAL

Social networking sites like *LinkedIn* and *Facebook* are great business networking tools. But if the only contact you have with your network is through the occasional email and things you post on social networking sites, you won't develop much of a connection with them. However, if you also make the effort to reach out with an occasional phone call or even face-to-face meeting, you'll develop much more robust relationships. That doesn't mean you have to set up meetings with every single member of your network; you can limit these special efforts to your top-tier contacts.

Social Media Networking

LinkedIn is a business-centric social media site that's designed to make it easy for you to build a business network. It also hosts mentoring groups and provides useful articles and guides. Well-known social networking sites, like *Facebook* and *Twitter*, are also excellent places to look for new connections.

Many of your network contacts will likely be located far away, which rules out taking them out for coffee. However, you can set up virtual meetings using one of the many meeting software programs. Such meetings can be nearly as effective as in-person ones when building connections with your more far-flung contacts.

DO MORE THAN SHOW UP

Some salespeople attend a lot of network events and collect business cards, and yet never really establish a business network. Other salespeople only go to the occasional event yet make many contacts each time. What's the difference? Just appearing and gathering handfuls of business cards isn't enough. In fact, if that's all you're doing, you may as well not be going to those events at all. Once again, think of networking as relationship building. You can't hope to develop any kind of relationship without putting some effort into it.

NOURISH YOUR CONTACTS

Network contacts are people too. You can't just ignore them for long periods of time, then all at once reach out to them and expect them to respond. It's critical to at least touch base with each of your contacts regularly. One good way to do this is to track important events in your contacts' lives and send an email or a brief note recognizing those events.

For example, you could send an email on a contact's birthday, the anniversary of the day you first met him, or a holiday. If you can include some information that will be of interest to him or comment on a recent post he made, that's even better.

NETWORKING EVENTS

How to Work the Room

Networking events are time-consuming, but they also provide the ultimate opportunity for meeting and greeting new network contacts. Because these events give you the chance to meet people face-to-face, you can form an immediate emotional connection that can take months or years to develop with someone you communicate with only online.

Before you sign up for an event, study the agenda closely. Some networking events are wonderful places to meet new contacts, while others are complete duds. Since you'll typically be investing several hours of your time to attend such an event, you'll want to get enough of a feel for it in advance that you can be reasonably sure you won't be wasting your time. Ask the event organizers if they can give you a list of attendees before you sign up—if you see at least a few attendees you'd like to meet, you'll know that the event will be worth attending.

When you go to a networking event, you're there to network. Should be obvious, right? Regrettably, some of the people who attend such events have either no desire to network (maybe they are there only because their sales managers made them attend) or no idea how to do it. Do your best to avoid those people, and instead focus on the ones who are serious about networking.

Listen more than you speak. Part of networking is demonstrating to people that you would be a good person to include in *their* network. Making a sincere effort to understand the other person's needs and listen to what he is telling you will go far toward showing people that you would be a great choice for an ongoing business relationship.

IT'S WORDS AND BODY LANGUAGE

Remember that communicating isn't only about the words that you speak. Your body language has a much greater effect on how people perceive you than your choice of words. Sustain eye contact and tip your head a little bit toward the person who is speaking to you to demonstrate your interest. Roving eyes indicate roving attention, which will quickly alienate someone who's trying to talk to you.

Be considerate about approaching someone. Don't interrupt in the middle of someone else's conversation, even if you are anxious to meet one of the people involved. Wait until the person is by herself or at least not in the midst of a conversation before introducing yourself. It's also not a good idea to approach someone who's on her way to the restroom—wait for her to come back instead. When you approach a large group of people, try to edge yourself into the conversation instead of barging in on them. Take a minute or two to stand next to the group and make eye contact with each person before you start speaking.

On the other hand, don't wait for people to approach you. You don't expect prospects to approach you—you have to make the first move to go to them. Networking requires a comparable attitude. To build a strong network, you have to take control of things and take the initiative about approaching people. Set an ambitious target—perhaps meeting fifty new people at the event—and take that goal seriously.

At least one person, and probably a lot more than one, will ask you what you do for a living. You'll want to have a good, interesting answer ready, because freezing up or babbling incoherently will not exactly make a great impression. Your answer should be about ten to fifteen seconds long and should pique the listener's interest without being pushy or sounding too much like a salesperson. The idea is to tell the other person just enough about your work to intrigue them, without going into so much detail that you bore them instead.

Be a business card ninja. Exchanging business cards at an event is almost an art form. The idea is to be clever and subtle about making the exchange while passing along the impression that you value the other person's card highly. Some specifics: keep your cards handy; write your cell phone number on the back just before you hand the card to someone; and when you receive someone else's card, immediately write something he said on the back to demonstrate to him that you take his advice seriously.

Business Cards

Bring a lot of business cards—at least two or three times as many as you think you're likely to hand out. Having leftover cards is no problem, but you'll be kicking yourself if you run out of cards during the event. Don't forget to bring several pens!

You can show immediately what a helpful person you are by introducing a new acquaintance to someone you've already met earlier in the event. That helps those people to grow their own networks—something that is clearly important to them or they wouldn't be there. It can also bring about some interesting conversations that could even help you out in some way.

Finally, once the event is over, be sure to follow up with every one of your potential new contacts. Not all of these meetings will result in a useful addition to your network, but at least some of the people you meet will likely be valuable resources in the future.

BUILDING A NETWORK

Starting from Scratch

The most challenging part of networking is connecting with your first few contacts. Once you have the start of a network, all you have to do is take care of it and you'll be able to make it grow indefinitely.

The first step in developing a network is determining who you want to include in it. Make a list of your top potential contacts, just as you might select potential prospects for a sales call. Your ideal contact list should consist of people who can be valuable over the long term. Some of those contacts may be potential prospects, but don't limit yourself solely to sales targets. Networking contacts can be useful in a number of other ways—they might be people who can connect you with major prospects, people who can furnish useful information on different topics, or even people who might provide access to your dream job.

If you don't know who to look for, begin with the company names and then work inward. Find people who work for that company and target the ones whose job titles suggest that they might be the right people for you to approach. If you can't get to the ideal person right away, begin with someone else who works for that company. Once you've made him a part of your network, he can help you connect with your ultimate contact at that company.

Don't go after contacts who can't be of use to you in some way. Maintaining a network can be time-consuming, and if you're wasting a lot of time with contacts who can't really help you, you're misusing that time. You can use a little more latitude in qualifying network contacts than you would in qualifying sales leads, as it's possible that someone you develop as a contact now will be an enormous help to you in a year or two. Keep a list of your contacts that includes the ways in which they're helpful to you, and if someone on your list can no longer be of help to you, take him out of your network.

INTRODUCE YOURSELF

After you've identified and qualified a prospective contact, your next step is to introduce yourself. Don't wait for her to come to you, as many people are reluctant to be the first to approach—particularly when it comes to introducing themselves to a total stranger. As a salesperson, you have a big advantage in that you are far more comfortable with initiating contact. After you've made a few hundred cold calls, introducing yourself to people at a local mixer or on *Facebook* will be a snap.

First Impressions

Making a good first impression is vital, particularly if you're pursuing a relationship with someone who already has a strong network or who is in a powerful position. The first two minutes of dialogue or the first online message will set the tone for your entire relationship.

Your initial conversation is your first and possibly only chance to create rapport with a prospective contact. To begin, try to help the other person relax. Smile, make eye contact, be friendly, and use positive body language. If you're communicating online, make use of emoticons to symbolize body language and lighten up the conversation.

Next, ask a couple of questions, and use active listening to show that you're interested in what he is saying. If possible, this initial conversation should be all about the other person. If there's an opportunity, don't hesitate to say something briefly about how you can add value for him, but mostly you should be listening and asking questions rather than speaking. After a few minutes of conversation, it's time to wrap things up as naturally as possible. One good way to end the conversation in a positive way is to suggest that the two of you chat again at a specific later date.

Bear in mind throughout this process that your network contacts aren't just useful resources; they're *people* who will expect you to be a resource in turn. If you wish to include someone in your network, you have to show him how he can benefit from networking with you, just as you would with a prospect. The best way to induce a contact to join your network is to do something for him right away. It could be something small, like introducing him to someone else you know or sending him a useful article. If you choose a new network contact who happens to be located nearby, you could invite him out for coffee. The idea is to demonstrate that you can be helpful or at least pleasant company.

LEARN ABOUT YOUR CONTACTS

As you become better acquainted with your new contacts, get to know what their interests are. You can often find hobbies and so forth mentioned on social media pages, especially on *Facebook*. Knowing these personal details will make it much easier for you to return the favor when someone helps you. It will also make your contacts feel good about you because they'll recognize that you're paying attention to their likes and dislikes.

When you've just established your network, don't even consider asking your contacts for favors. You have to spend some time getting acquainted with them and doing favors for them first. If someone offers to help in some way, that's great, but don't ask until you have developed a track record of being helpful. And as your network evolves, continue to do at least two or three favors for every one you ask for. That will keep your contacts happy and your network strong.

COMMON NETWORKING MISTAKES

Treat Your Contacts with Respect

Some salespeople argue that networking is a waste of time, and indeed it can be when it's not done right. Networking can give your sales a significant boost and improve other aspects of your life as well—but not if you waste your time and energy with these common blunders.

MOVING TOO FAST

A networking event or meeting isn't the time to break out your sales pitch. The objective is to get to know people and make contacts, not sales. If you attempt to close sales at the event itself, you'll come across as pushy, and most of the people you encounter will be reluctant to do business with you. Get business cards or contact information from everyone who seems to be a juicy resource, and you can follow up with them later at your leisure.

NOT MOVING FAST ENOUGH

A lot of new salespeople going to their first networking event stand around waiting for people to approach them and introduce themselves. To make your time there as productive as possible, take the initiative and approach others. Consider it a chance to practice your people skills in a nonthreatening environment.

NOT HAVING A GOAL

You always need to have a plan of attack before tackling any networking activity. This can be something as simple as "Send out ten *LinkedIn* invitations per week." After all, if you don't know what your goal is, you're not likely to meet it. A goal can help keep you motivated when your initial surge of enthusiasm starts to wear off.

LOOKING IN THE WRONG PLACES

Different types of salespeople are looking for different types of network contacts. If you go to events at which none of the attendees has the potential to be a useful resource, you won't accomplish anything. Similarly, spending a lot of time on a social media platform that doesn't have the kinds of contacts you're looking for is just a waste.

NOT LISTENING

Salespeople are often social extroverts who enjoy monopolizing the conversation. To be effective, a salesperson must overcome this tendency sufficiently to allow the other party do her share of the talking. Try to keep your talking to less than half the time. If you're at a lunch or dinner event, watch your partner's plate—if she's finished most of her meal and you've hardly eaten any, you are talking far too much. The same goes for an exchange of messages, whether by email, chat, or social media; ask questions and express interest to draw out the other person as much as you can.

NOT QUALIFYING

Develop some questions that will help you to determine whether or not a new contact is a likely resource. If he's not a fit for you, he may still be helpful as a way to reach other, more useful people, but you won't want to spend a lot of time cultivating such secondary contacts.

NOT HAVING AN ELEVATOR SPEECH

An elevator speech is a brief explanation of what you do, complete with a benefits statement. It's highly useful at networking events where you'll meet a lot of different people very quickly. The perfect elevator speech is short, is clearly stated, and motivates the listener to say, "Tell me more." A good elevator speech is also quite useful for communicating online. Try writing one that's short enough to fit into a single tweet.

Online Body Language

When you're communicating online, the other person generally can't see you. The good news is that he won't know if you roll your eyes at him, but the bad news is he may misunderstand a joke or statement you make. Emoticons can help you avoid such misunderstandings.

BAD BODY LANGUAGE

A lot of people who attend networking events run around handing out cards and rushing away immediately to the next contact. When you encounter someone at an event, allow time to shake her hand, make eye contact, and have at least a short conversation. Your body language should let her know that you're interested in what she is saying. Don't be constantly looking over her shoulder for the next potential contact.

NOT FOLLOWING UP

After you've gathered all those names and business cards from your latest networking event, don't put them in a desk drawer and forget about them. Get in touch with potential contacts as soon as you can after the event and schedule times to meet. If you can, send them warm leads or something else they might find useful, like newspaper clippings related to their business. This will likely encourage your new contacts to do the same for you. It's also good manners to respond quickly to any invites you get through *LinkedIn* or other social media sites.

SOCIAL MEDIA NETWORKING

Twitter, *LinkedIn*, and More

With such a variety of social media networks out there, it can be challenging to figure out which one—or two, or three—is best for your needs. Don't confine yourself to the ones you know best; search and experiment and get to know them. Each of the social networks has its own strengths and weaknesses, so before you decide which one to focus on you need to figure out how you want to use it, and what you'd like to get out of it. Here we'll talk about some of the more popular ones, but in the next few years, more will emerge, and some of them may work better for you.

FACEBOOK

Facebook is the largest social media network, with well over two billion monthly active users. It has a lot of tools that allow users to create events, craft and deploy targeted ads, share files such as images and videos, and more. *Facebook*'s strengths are building and maintaining relationships between users. It's a terrific place to use if you wish to add value for prospects and customers alike. You can also use *Facebook* to assert yourself on your own terms, displaying your personality clearly rather than coming across as another faceless corporate entity.

TWITTER

With only 280 characters available per message, you have to keep your tweets short and sweet. On the other hand, since short responses are obligatory, keeping up with *Twitter* can be much less time-consuming than maintaining other social network pages. Of course, you can also get caught up in conversations and unexpectedly discover that hours have passed. *Twitter* is a great place to broadcast information about promotions, events, and news that might interest prospects and customers. You can also put an intriguing tweet out there to get conversations started between your followers.

LINKEDIN

The preeminent B2B networking site, *LinkedIn* is an ideal place to do some business networking. You can also use it to get in touch with high-level decision-makers you've had difficulty reaching in the past. Joining the right *LinkedIn* groups can also help validate you as a subject matter expert, which can result in prospects actually coming to you for advice.

YOUTUBE

While not as suitable for direct contact as the three social media platforms listed previously, *YouTube* can be an effective way to arouse the interest of new prospects. One commonly used approach is to record yourself describing how to do something that your prospects would want to know about. For business purposes, short videos are usually the most effective, so set yourself a limit of one to two minutes. If you include the relevant keywords, your video will have a very good chance of coming up on *Google* when your prospects do a search on the subject.

Depending on how much time you want to allocate to social media, you may want to use just one social media platform or extend your efforts to multiple networks. If you choose only one, you have to decide what your highest priority is and then select the social media network that is best suited to your priority. For example, if most of your customers are consumers and you want to keep them interested and happy, *Facebook* is probably the best choice. However, if your top priority is business networking, you'll likely prefer *LinkedIn*.

A Quick Way to Get More Followers

In your email signature line, include links to your social media accounts. That way, it's easy for contacts and customers to access your posts and become followers. You can also add your social media account information to your business cards.

Bear in mind, too, that different social media platforms require different update frequencies. *Twitter* generally moves the fastest, and you'll probably want to post several times each day if you can. Luckily, there are tools that enable you to draft tweets in advance and automatically post them later. On the other hand, on *LinkedIn* you can be quite active just by posting a couple of times per week.

KEEP IT PROFESSIONAL

Whatever network you select, remember to always keep things professional. Sometimes that can be difficult, especially if a former customer is criticizing you on *Facebook*, but it's absolutely mandatory. Bear in mind that everything you post on the Internet will be out there forever, so before you submit something, ask yourself if you want it to be available for anyone to read in the future.

Once you've chosen the best social media network for your needs, the following tips will help you get the most from the time you invest in it.

Stay Current

Review your profiles on a regular basis to make sure they're up-to-date. The first thing a new contact will probably do is read your profile, and if it contains a lot of outdated information and non-functional links, she will probably not want to add you to her network.

Change It Up

Don't enter exactly the same information on every one of your social networking accounts at the same time. A lot of your followers are likely to be reading your accounts across multiple social media platforms, so in essence you'll be spamming them each time. Rather, mix up your posts somewhat so they'll discover a variety of different things when they follow you in more than one place.

Ratio of Followers to Followed

Maintain a pretty close ratio of followers to followed accounts. Having many more followers than followed accounts makes you seem to be someone who doesn't like to reciprocate, but having many more followed accounts than followers looks like you don't have anything to say.

Keep It in Balance

Don't get carried away. If you notice that you're spending too much time reading and posting on social media sites, budget your online time. Social media is a great sales tool, but you can't neglect your other sales activities and still hope to succeed.

Read Posts

Pay attention to your contacts' posts. Although many of your posts ought to be about you, be certain to include mentions of interesting news or events or that your contacts have shared with you. Take the time to respond to your contacts directly when they post something arresting.

Do for Others

Reward your contacts ahead of time. When you can, do at least one favor for a social media contact before you ask her to do something for you.

Update

Post updates on a regular basis. If you don't have anything exciting to share, try posting an interesting quote or put out a question to your contacts. This will often initiate a discussion.

CHAPTER 10
QUOTAS AND SALES SLUMPS

Sales is a "what have you done for me lately" kind of career. Salespeople are expected to hit their quotas—or, better yet, exceed them—month after month and year after year. No matter how well you did last month, if your sales start to slide this month, you'll definitely be hearing from your sales manager. The surest way to keep your numbers consistent is to draw up a plan and set your goals before each quota cycle begins. Of course, no matter how well you plan, there will be the occasional week or month when you just can't seem to sell anything, and getting out of those sales slumps quickly requires a particular mindset. As you struggle to hit a tricky quota, increasing the amount of business you do with your existing customers (known as "wallet share," discussed later in this chapter) can be a useful way to grab some extra sales. Recessions make selling tougher for just about everyone; you'll need to know how to weather these economic storms with grace. Finally, if you believe that your quotas are unreachable and unfair, get your entire sales team together and work on convincing management of that fact.

HOW SALES QUOTAS WORK

Getting with the Program

A quota, or sales goal, is the amount of revenue that a salesperson is expected to generate within a given period of time. Virtually all companies set quotas for their salespeople, because a quota both ensures that each salesperson knows what is expected of him and is the easiest way to calculate what commissions are due for that salesperson.

Quotas can take a wide variety of forms. A small company with a few salespeople and one or two products to sell will probably set a very simple quota—for example, the goal might be for each salesperson to sell $60,000 worth of products during each calendar quarter, with no preference as to how much of each product a salesperson sells. However, a large company with thousands of sales reps and a lot of different services or products might set a very complicated quota involving different targets for different products—ten new subscribers to a certain service, twenty units of a certain product, $10,000 worth of add-on services, and so forth.

If a large company has offices spread out across a wide area, the goals may be set differently for each office depending on the territory's perceived potential. As a result, an office that customarily makes a lot of sales and has a great deal of market potential will have higher goals for its salespeople than one in an area with few likely customers.

Quotas may be set for different periods of time, ranging anywhere from weekly to yearly, but monthly or quarterly quotas are the most common. These relatively long quota periods give salespeople plenty of time to tailor their sales strategies to their goals and formulate a sales plan. Quarterly quotas in particular also allow companies to take the seasonal fluctuations of a product into consideration. If a specific product sells much better in winter than in summer, the company can set a higher quota in Q1 than it does in Q3 and still keep up revenue generation without putting too much pressure on the sales team.

Some quotas also factor in whether you're selling to new customers or existing ones. Most companies want to hit a certain balance between these two types of sales. Selling additional products and services to existing customers makes them more likely to stay with your company in the long term, since the more they own, the more of a hassle it would be for them to switch providers. On the other hand, every company needs an ongoing flow of new customers in order to grow and to replace those customers who do leave. Sales quotas often try to balance these two needs by specifying that a certain percentage of sales must come from new customers.

Sales executives will usually use projections of how their industry will be doing in the near future combined with historical data to determine how to set sales quotas. Unfortunately, even the best forecasting models can be highly inaccurate, particularly when the marketplace experiences sudden and unexpected changes. For example, if a particular industry is shaken by a scandal or if new technology renders a particular product obsolete, the salespeople are unlikely to meet quotas that did not take those issues into consideration. In situations like these a sales manager should ideally adjust how he pays out commissions to relieve some of the sales team's distress, assuming that those salespeople did a reasonable job given the circumstances.

Commissions are generally tied to quotas in some way. Sometimes it's a direct correlation, such as a commission structure that returns 5 percent for every unit sold under quota and 10 percent after the salesperson meets her quota. In other situations companies might establish commissions based on mathematical calculations that consider various factors, such as the salesperson's level of performance in selling many different products. Usually, tying sales commissions to the amount of revenue that a salesperson brings in is a good way to compensate the salesperson fairly while keeping that compensation in line with how much money the company gained from her efforts.

Some sales jobs have a "base plus commission" compensation structure. These jobs pay a certain base amount—say, $40,000 per year—plus a commission on top of that. If you have a sales job that falls into that category, you'll receive your base salary regardless of whether or not you hit your quotas. However, you may not get any commissions at all unless you meet or exceed your goals. If you're not sure how your own compensation structure works, ask your sales manager to clarify for you.

Compensation Structures

A sales job with a base plus commission compensation structure is reassuring for new salespeople, since you're guaranteed at least some income even if you never make a sale. However, pure commission sales jobs end up paying more for good performers, so experienced salespeople often prefer those jobs.

As a general rule many sales experts say that a quota is fair if approximately 80 percent of the salespeople on the team can meet it during each quota period. If less than 80 percent of the sales team is attaining their quota most of the time, the numbers need to be adjusted downward—but if the whole team consistently meets or exceeds their quota, then the quota needs to adjusted upward to provide them with a greater challenge.

STARTING A NEW SALES PERIOD

How to Start Strong

Whether your quota cycle runs monthly, quarterly, or over some other time frame, starting out right can have an enormous impact on how well you do over the entire period.

The first thing to do before any quota cycle begins is to decide on your goals. Obviously, your quota will affect the goals you set, but you don't have to use the quota as your ultimate goal or even as a goal at all. In fact, having multiple goals is usually the most effective self-motivation strategy. For example, you might have a minimum goal of hitting your assigned quota and a stretch goal of selling fifty units over your quota.

If you have a different quota for every product or service you sell, then you don't have to obsess over setting specific goals for each product; in that situation you might use an overall goal that's based on a percentage of whatever your specific goals are. For example, your stretch goal might be selling 10 percent over whatever your quota is for each product.

You can usually use your performance in the last quota cycle as a baseline for setting your goal for the upcoming period. For example, if you didn't quite hit your quota during the last sales period, your goal might be to hit your quota this time. But if you made your quota with ease, your minimum goal might be to exceed your quota by 5 percent, and your stretch goal might be to exceed it by an even higher percentage.

Setting your minimum and stretch goals right from the beginning is crucial to succeeding because without a goal, you won't have a target to shoot for as you plow through the month or quarter to come.

For example, if you set your goals before the quota period begins, you'll be able to set mini-goals at various points to keep yourself on track. If your quota cycle is a quarterly one and your goal is to sell 300 units, your mini-goal would be selling 100 units each month. Using this system, if you sold only 75 units during the first month of the quarter, you'd know right away that you're falling behind on your quarterly goal and need to make some extra sales next month to catch up.

When used in combination with your sales metrics, your sales period goal can help you determine exactly which sales activities you need to complete in order to succeed. If your goal is to sell 100 units per month and you know from reviewing your past metrics that you close a sale with about 25 percent of your leads, that means you'll need to cold call at least 400 leads during the month. Let's say there are twenty-three working days in the current month. In that case you'll need to make eighteen cold calls per day to have a good chance of reaching your goal.

Sales Metrics

Your sales metrics are your trackable performance indicators. The number of cold calls you make, referrals you get, appointments you schedule, and sales you close are all important metrics. Knowing your metrics will tell you what tasks you need to do in order to hit your quota.

Of course, your performance in a given week or month won't always match your average performances. You might have a run of bad luck and find that you are closing only 15 percent of your leads this month. However, if you're tracking your performance as you go along, you'll know before it's too late that you're not quite making the numbers you expected, and can work some extra cold calls into your schedule to make up the difference. Or you can try something a little different, like running a sales campaign, to drum up a few extra prospects and get yourself back on track.

When you're deciding how to plan out your sales activities for the day, week, and so on, aim for your stretch goal rather than your minimum goal. That way, if you do perform below your average, you'll still have a decent shot at making at least your minimum goal. Assuming your minimum goal is at or above your quota, you'll be more likely to get a nice commission check even in underperforming months.

If you're just coming off of a really bad month or quarter in which you failed to hit your quota, you'll be under some extra pressure to make up for that failure in the next period. The first thing to do is to list the activities you'll be doing to achieve or surpass your sales goals. It's always wise to have a sales plan, but if you're coming out of a difficult period, then having a plan is even more critical. The system you were using before didn't work very successfully, so you need to develop a new one before you do any more selling.

One thing that you need to include in your sales plan is a sub-plan that addresses prospecting activities. Prospecting is what will determine if your sales efforts are successful. If you don't put enough effort into prospecting, you won't have sufficient leads flowing into your sales pipeline—which means that no matter how well you sell, you probably won't close enough sales. Because many salespeople shrink from cold calling, it's tempting to put off prospecting whenever you can. You can reduce your procrastination by scheduling a certain period of time during which you'll dedicate yourself entirely to cold calling. This may mean setting aside an hour every day, or picking a multi-hour period once a week—whatever works best for you.

Finally, polish your lead qualification process. You mustn't waste time on bad leads if you're to improve your performance. Go through the questions that you've been using to qualify leads, and compare them to your best current customers. Do those questions focus on the characteristics that your very best customers share? If not, discard any irrelevant questions and add others that will help identify bad or weak leads. As a result you will have fewer prospects, but all of those prospects will be optimal potential customers. That means you'll have more time and energy to put into them, which will probably result in bigger and better sales.

GETTING OUT OF A SALES SLUMP

First, Don't Panic

If your sales have been way down for days and you're beginning to feel like you'll never close another sale, don't panic. You may be able to escape your current slump with the following tactics.

EXAMINE THE "WHY"

Before you can solve the problem, you need to determine what it is. There are two possible kinds of causes: external and internal. External causes are those that are imposed upon you from the outside, like industry problems or economic slowdowns. They will generally affect your coworkers' numbers as well as your own. However, if your sales are plunging and the rest of your team is doing fine, the cause is probably internal.

FIND WAYS TO MANAGE EXTERNAL CAUSES

By their very nature, external problems are beyond your control. For example, if your industry or company has recently received a lot of bad press, there will be an impact on your sales no matter what you do. However, you can lessen the impact by addressing the issue directly. Now is the time to develop a new pitch that focuses directly on the problem. If it's a universal issue, such as a recession, write a pitch that demonstrates how your service or product can help. If it's a company- or industry-wide problem, talk about what your company is doing to address it. Your friends in the PR department, if you have some, can probably help you come up with some good talking points to use.

RESOLVE INTERNAL CAUSES

Sales is largely emotion-based, so it's not unexpected that your personal life may affect your performance. Or possibly you've been depending too long on the same list of leads or your pitch has gotten stale; if you realize you are bored with your own pitch, prospects will notice! Whatever the reason, getting out of your comfort zone can help revitalize your emotional outlook. If cold calling is your primary strategy, try turning to social networking tools like *Twitter* and *Facebook*. If you usually depend on a lot of e-marketing, get out of the office and do some door-to-door calling. Write a new pitch that concentrates on completely different features of the product. Address a totally new segment of the market. By making fundamental changes to your technique, you can get your mind working and generate some excitement and energy.

Once you have a plan of action, the next step is to really crank up your sales activities. If you would usually make twenty cold calls per day, make forty or fifty instead. Or you could simply keep calling until you manage to make five appointments, even if that means you spend ten hours on the phone that day. Communicate with all your existing customers and see if they can provide some referrals or even if you can upsell them new products.

While you're making all those cold calls, don't forget to qualify. The more meticulous you are about qualifying prospects, the less time you'll waste on someone who can't buy from you. It also saves time when you confirm up front that the person you're speaking with has the authority to buy. That way, you can get in front of the decision-maker faster. The time you spend qualifying a prospect will be more than made up for by the time you save not making unnecessary presentations.

Qualifying for Quality

When you're generating sale after sale, you can afford to be picky about leads and solicit only the ones you think will be major customers, a.k.a. whales. But when you're stuck in a slump, grab every qualified prospect you can.

It's also wise to spend a little extra time prepping for each sales appointment you make. The more prepared you are before a sales presentation, the easier it will be. That's critical during a sales slump, when you're probably already feeling a bit apprehensive. If you have a rock-solid presentation, know how to respond to all the common objections, have a lot of sales questions prepared in advance, and have your close well planned, you'll feel far more secure. And that feeling of security will be obvious to your prospects. They'll feel safer about buying from a confident salesperson than from one whose body language projects "desperate."

When you're desperate to close more sales, it's easy to submit to the urge to offer discounts and special offers—whatever it takes to close a sale. But that method will cost you a lot more money than it will get you. Giving a big discount at the first opportunity tells a prospect that you're an easy mark, and he'll keep on pushing as a customer, insisting on special treatment forever. And once you start offering discounts, it becomes a habit that's hard to break. You'll do much better to hold the line and offer non-monetary perks if you absolutely have to.

Give each new sales method you try at least a few days before you give up on it. If you're still not seeing any results, then set it aside and try something else. If you do start to get positive results from a particular strategy, do even more of it! Persistence and stubbornness are the keys to beating a bad sales slump.

BUILDING WALLET SHARE

Selling to Your Existing Customers

Whether you're struggling to get out of a slump or trying to hit a tricky quota, selling to existing customers can be a boon. Building wallet share can be a good thing both for you and for your company.

Wallet share is a way of measuring how much business you're doing with a particular customer. Your company has a high wallet share with a customer who owns and uses several of your products or services, while a customer who owns only one product made by your company and gets a number of other products from your competitors would represent a low wallet share.

A high wallet share is desirable for a number of reasons. First and most obvious, higher wallet share means that you've sold a customer a lot of your products, which equals more sales for you and more revenue for your employer. Second, the more of your products a particular customer owns, the "stickier" he is. In other words, he's less likely to give up on you and move on to a competitor. And third, it's much easier to sell to an existing customer than it is to sell to a new prospect. If you're not selling multiple products to your customers, you're ignoring the opportunity to close some very easy deals.

The simplest way to build wallet share is to cross-sell. When you make a sale to a prospect, also mention one or more other products that would be an equally good fit for that prospect. You might even offer a discount or some other incentive for buying more than one product at once. Upselling is another way to build wallet share. This means selling add-on products or services that are designed to accompany a main product. Common upsell options include maintenance agreements, warranties, and parts. For example, if you sell laser printers, extra toner cartridges would be a natural upsell.

The initial sale is not the only time to build wallet share with your customers. In fact, as your company adds new product lines or rolls out new models, you should let your customers know about these updates and suggest that they take the opportunity to upgrade their existing products. Many customers will be quite pleased with you for keeping them up-to-date on the newest offerings and will be happy to buy the brand-new model every year or two.

Staying In Touch

It's best to reach out to existing customers roughly every three to six months. That gives you a chance to resolve any issues before they cause the customer to leave, as well as a great opportunity to sell her something.

When you reach out to an existing customer with the intention of upselling or cross-selling to him, don't start pitching the second you hear the customer's voice. After all, you wouldn't try to sell a product over the phone to a brand-new prospect—you'd set up an appointment to meet with him and *then* start pitching. If you just blurt out your sales pitch to an existing customer over the phone, he's likely to turn you down without really listening to what you have to say.

Instead of jumping straight into your sales pitch, start out by asking the customer how things are working out with his current products. Really dig for information and find out if he has any problems or unresolved questions. You need to get those issues fixed before you can introduce any new products. If there are existing problems, that can actually help you build wallet share because taking the time to ask and then helping the customer resolve those issues will make him very grateful.

Once you've resolved any existing problems, you can introduce the primary reason for your call. One very effective way to open the subject is by offering to conduct an account review. If he asks what you mean by that, tell him that it's a service you offer to be sure that every customer is getting the most possible benefits from the product or service.

During your account review ask questions about how the customer is using the product, what he likes and dislikes about it, and what other related products he uses. This is precisely the information you need to make an intelligent recommendation about other products that might work for him. When you follow up your account review by saying something like, "Based on what we've discussed today, product X can be extremely useful for you. It will resolve issues Y and Z," you'll have an excellent shot at managing the sale.

Another way to meet with existing customers is to conduct an event once or twice a year. Customers are often annoyed that new customers qualify for special deals while existing ones don't. You can make a point of reversing this trend with a "customer appreciation day," an event at which you offer coupons, discounts, small gifts, entertainment, food, prizes, and whatever else you can think of. Make sure to grab business cards or otherwise collect contact information from attendees (perhaps by holding a raffle) so that you can follow up later and see about closing a sale or two.

SELLING DURING A RECESSION

Tough Times Are Tough for Salespeople

All economies, whether local, national, or global, have their ups and downs. When the economies that affect you are doing well, the usual result is a seller's market—that is to say, demand is high, so it's comparatively easy to sell your product. When your economy is low, though, watch out—you're now in a buyer's market, with low demand and a lot of competitors working at selling to your prospects.

Economic problems are not the only reason for a buyer's market. If your company is suffering from a major difficulty—for example, a competing company that cuts its prices or an industry-wide scandal that frightens away prospective buyers—you may also find yourself working hard for every sale. A buyer's market is challenging for salespeople because circumstances out of their control have suddenly made their job much more difficult. As most salespeople are very focused on keeping control, this kind of situation can produce frustration completely out of proportion to its actual impact.

You can't make changes to the economy or the industry, but you can change your reaction to it. Taking the proper action will make it much easier for you to sell successfully under these circumstances.

First, take a good look at your sales methodology, from prospecting all the way to closing the sale. There are probably things you can do to tighten up your sales strategies and help them become more effective. Usually, the worse a buyer's market gets, the more leads you'll have to approach to end up with the necessary number of closes. That means that you have to increase your cold calling and other prospecting processes to get meetings with as many leads as possible. If your usual goal is one hundred cold calls each week, set aside the time for 150 cold calls for the next three weeks, and then assess how many of those calls you succeeded in turning into appointments. If you still don't have enough appointments, increase the number of calls to 200 per week next time.

Next, if the buyer's market is caused by a far-reaching problem, like a recession, your prospects are going to be feeling the effect of it as well. They will probably be overworked and on edge just from the stress of financial worries and staying on top of their own jobs. Rewrite your sales presentation to emphasize security, comfort, and helpfulness. Because your prospects are frightened, presenting yourself as someone who can help them with their problems will be very attractive to them. And as you're modifying your presentation, cut the length by at least 25 percent—busy prospects will be less willing to sit through a long presentation.

Prospects often get a lot more price-conscious during tough times, which means you'll likely get a lot of requests for discounts. When you get such a request, say something like, "We don't discount because our standard price is already the best possible price we can offer."

You Really Don't Want Price-Focused Customers

Prospects who absolutely refuse to do business with you unless you lower the price will be terrible customers. In most cases your best bet is to walk away from those sales. Super cost-conscious customers are high-maintenance and will harass you constantly looking for a better deal.

If a prospect keeps pushing for a discount, you should try to uncover exactly why she thinks your product is overpriced. She may be comparing it to a competitor's product that doesn't have the same capabilities, or perhaps she last shopped for a similar product many years ago and doesn't realize that prices have gone up since.

Sometimes a prospect wants to buy but truly feels that he can't afford to pay your price. In that case you can sometimes help him to find a way. It may be that he doesn't have the money now but will be able to squeeze the purchase into next month's budget. Or you might be able to offer an extended payment plan, where the prospect pays full price but does it in installments.

If you're in B2B sales, you're likely to find yourself facing a more complicated purchasing process, especially if you're selling high-end, expensive services and products. Like consumers, businesses respond to financial challenges by curtailing purchases. You may discover that instead of convincing one CEO or purchasing officer, you now have to make your presentation to an entire buying committee. And if your decision-maker(s) have to get approval from someone even higher up the ladder, then the whole sales process will take much longer. That means that creating a solid sales plan is more important than ever. If the length of your average sales cycle doubles during a buyer's market, you must take that into consideration when you're planning your sales activities.

Finally, a difficult marketplace is a terrific chance to concentrate some effort on your existing customers. After all, if you can't create as many new customers as you usually do, the only way to solve the problem is to capture more market share through your current customers. That means customer service ought to be a major priority. If you've taken good care of your existing customers, they should have a pretty high level of trust in you—and as a result they'll be more inclined to consider upgrading their current product or even purchasing a few additional ones.

RESOLVING QUOTA PROBLEMS

If Your Quota Is Out of Reach

Just about every salesperson, no matter how talented, has experienced that disheartening feeling of being seriously behind on sales quotas. When you first realize how behind you are, it's very easy to panic—especially if your sales manager is on your back (because *he* has quotas too!).

But pushing the panic button is not the answer. The best way to deal with this situation is to work smarter and faster than you already are. You're unlikely to have time to develop enough cold leads to get out of trouble, although flooding your pipeline will definitely reduce the chance of encountering this kind of problem in the next quota cycle. But when your deadline is coming on fast and you're really behind, there's only one possible solution—short-circuiting the usual sales cycle.

Every company and every industry has a certain rhythm based on the length of the sales cycle. Some salespeople within the same company may have slightly longer or shorter sales cycles, but a basic consistency exists due to the nature of the sales team's customer base and product. If you have to shorten that cycle radically, you'll need to be creative in your approach.

The place to start in these desperate moments is with your existing customers. Hopefully, you have been keeping in touch with them, helping them resolve any issues, and banking some goodwill credit. If that's the case, now is the time to draw on that credit! Phone them one by one and ask for referrals. Depending on the sales goals and the nature of your product, you might also be able to upsell these existing customers or in some other way sell them additional products.

Next, this is the time to touch base with your stalled sales. Undoubtedly you have sales that simply seem to fade out in the middle of the cycle. Get in touch with those prospects and go all out with them. Find out what is blocking the sale, and if there's something you can do to remove the impediment. This doesn't necessarily mean offering a big discount—often a prospect's objection doesn't concern price. Nor does it mean being dishonest in some way with a prospect, which is highly unethical and will get you into far worse trouble than a simple missed quota.

Finally, get in contact with your networks. Most people have a number of support groups—business contacts, coworkers, family, friends, and so forth. Call in your favors from your neighbor who keeps borrowing your snowblower, your buddy in tech support, your uncle Joe, your groups on *LinkedIn*, and anyone else you can think of. If you are a member of a Chamber of Commerce or other local group, find out if they have any events in the next couple of days. If not, call up their office and ask them for help! They may have some ideas or even be able to guide you to a few people who are ready to buy.

Long-Term Fixes

If you miss your quota time and again, there's something fundamentally wrong with either your quota or your sales activities. In the latter case the best long-term fix is to crank up your prospecting. The more prospects you find, the more sales you can close—it's that simple.

Once the current crisis has passed (one way or another), it's time to determine how you ended up in that predicament to begin with. If you aren't already doing so, start reviewing your activities and see if there are areas in which you're not being productive. And of course, send thank-you notes or gifts to anyone who helped you out during your predicament.

If you believe your quota is simply impossible to hit, it's time to meet with your sales manager and discuss having it adjusted in the future. The best way to approach your manager is to get the team together and set up a group meeting.

Think of it as a sales call with your manager—in this case, a successful sale would be convincing him that your quota is unrealistically high. Before you go into the meeting, gather up all the proof you can find—your past performance numbers; evidence of external problems, such as economic slowdowns; and descriptions of your recent sales activities and their results. Be as specific as you possibly can. The idea is to show your manager that you did everything you could to make your quota, and you still couldn't hit it.

In a large company the sales quotas are usually set by someone in upper management. They'll often be determined on a company-wide level with adjustments based on region, area, and perhaps past sales performance at each location. In that case your sales manager won't be able to do much—although you should still go to him first so that he doesn't feel like you're going over his head. In fact, your sales manager is probably the best person to advise you on how to petition upper management for relief from your unrealistic quotas.

If the problem that has been affecting your sales numbers is temporary, then asking upper management to lower your quotas won't help much, because even if they agree, it will take time for the company to make the adjustments. But if the problem is an ongoing one, you have nothing to lose by lobbying for a change.

CHAPTER 11
MOVING INTO MANAGEMENT

Once you've been in sales for a while, you might start considering a hop up to management. Sales managers are frequently drawn from the ranks of top-performing salespeople, making it a natural career move. However, sales management does require quite a different mindset from sales itself. Before you make the leap, it's important to understand just what it is you're jumping into. In particular, the skills and traits that make someone an excellent sales manager are very different from the skills and traits cultivated by top salespeople, which can make the transition between these two roles rather rocky. For example, the single most important task for sales managers is coaching their sales teams, which generally isn't something that comes naturally to a person who's been in sales for a while. Sales managers face certain unavoidable challenges; once you know what to expect, though, you can work up some coping strategies to make these challenges much easier to deal with. Finally, your salespeople will be depending on you for help with challenges of their own. If you let them down, they won't be as successful—and you'll literally pay for this, since sales manager compensation is typically tied to how well the sales team produces.

SALES MANAGEMENT BASICS

Know This Before You Make the Leap

A sales manager is the person who is responsible for leading and directing a team of salespeople. A sales manager's responsibilities often but don't always include:

- Setting quotas
- Creating sales plans
- Assigning sales territories
- Mentoring the members of her sales team
- Assigning sales training
- Hiring and firing salespeople

In large companies sales quotas and plans are often set at the executive level, and a manager's main responsibility is to make sure that her salespeople meet those quotas.

Some sales managers transferred from other departments to sales, but most are highly successful salespeople who were promoted to a management role. When a company is ready to hire a new sales manager, usually they look first at the best salespeople on their existing sales teams. After all, the senior managers reason, those salespeople are already familiar with the sales process and the products and have experience in selling them effectively. Why not choose one of them to be in charge of the team?

As for the salespeople, many see moving into sales management as the obvious next step on the sales career path. At the very least it's a compliment to be offered a promotion, and it can be hard to refuse. But those salespeople often don't consider the problems that will arise from this change.

TRANSITION CHALLENGES

Transitioning from being a salesperson to a being a sales manager is difficult under any circumstances. The things that make someone a star salesperson are very different from the traits that make a great manager, and many salespeople who move on to a management role never come to grips with that fact. Everyone naturally resists change (that's one of the things that makes sales so challenging!), and a salesperson who has always had success in her job will be even less inclined to change something that's worked so well.

Sales Managers Have Quotas Too

Because a sales manager's compensation is, to a great extent, based on how many sales her team makes, she's very dependent on her salespeople. That can be really tough for former salespeople, who prefer to be in control. Sales management requires finding a balance between providing guidance and micromanaging.

When a salesperson is chosen from the sales team and is established as the new boss, matters become far more complex. The new manager was probably on the team for at least a couple of years. She's been working as a peer with people who now report to her. Many sales teams become very close, and salespeople often socialize on their own time, getting together to boast about big sales and complain about clueless bosses. At the same time sales teams can be highly competitive, and the individual salespeople may not trust each other. In the worst case they may even work to sabotage one another.

If you are close to the other members of your sales team, then moving into the role of being their manager will require that you alter that relationship in a significant way. As their boss, you will no longer be able to join them in making negative observations about the company or sharing office gossip. You should meet with each team member individually and explain your reasoning, so that they're not surprised by your change in attitude. But unless you are very fortunate, most of the friendships you have had with the salespeople will fade into simple professional relationships. If this disturbs you, don't accept the management position.

Consider it from the point of view of your former teammates. At one moment you are acting like a buddy, and the next you are responding very differently and refusing to gossip or share any juicy info you've picked up in your new position. Salespeople are just as opposed to change as everyone else, and even if they intellectually get why you're behaving differently, they could very well still resent it emotionally. Your salespeople may be thinking (or even saying to each other) something along the lines of, *Jane's promotion really went to her head. She doesn't want to hang around with us anymore and thinks she's better than we are now that she's a manager.*

If your sales team is very internally competitive, your problem will be different but just as difficult. Your new reports will be in the habit of thinking of you as a competitor or maybe even an enemy. But to function as a good manager, you have to get them to see you as an ally. It will take a while to build trust with each of your salespeople, so be patient. The most productive way to prove yourself to the team is to behave like the ally you want them to expect. Ask for suggestions and ideas and then implement them, if possible. If using an idea goes well, publicly give credit to the salesperson who gave you the idea, and take the blame if things fall through. That may not sound fair to you, but protecting your people is an essential part of your new job as a sales manager.

COMMUNICATION SKILLS

A sales manager needs outstanding communication skills to succeed. She must understand the sales plan, quota system, and compensation structure and be able to explain them clearly to her sales team. She must also know the needs of her salespeople and communicate those needs to the executive level. Since most salespeople already have well-honed communication skills, this likely won't be a problem for you—but be aware that moving into management doesn't mean you can quit selling; it just means you'll be selling internally (to upper management and to your sales team) rather than externally.

WHAT MAKES A GOOD SALES MANAGER?

Top Traits for Management Success

If you're still interested in becoming a sales manager now that you understand what to expect from the role, you'll need to consider whether you have the skills and talents necessary to thrive in such a position.

ARE YOU A TEAM PLAYER?

Many top salespeople prefer to work alone. They love the independent feeling of being on the phone or out on the road pursuing their own prospects. But sales management requires you to work closely with other people all day long. Not only do you have to work with your team, but you will also be expected to report back to upper management on a regular basis.

Being a coach for your salespeople is probably the most vital part of your job. This is your best tool for figuring out what's gone wrong with a salesperson and how to make it better. Usually, coaching involves the same types of skills as selling; it works best if you steer the salesperson toward identifying the problem and how to solve it rather than simply telling him what it is.

ARE YOU A GOOD LISTENER?

Good listening skills are just as important for a sales manager as for a salesperson. You have the ultimate responsibility for the success of your sales team. If you don't know what's going on with them, you won't realize that there are problems until they become really serious—at which point your own boss will probably be on your back. If you keep close tabs on your salespeople and encourage them to talk to you, you can become aware of problems while they're still minor.

ARE YOU COMFORTABLE RELYING ON OTHERS?

Salespeople are responsible for their own quotas. If a salesperson fails to make her sales, she might blame the economy or bad luck, but she can't blame her own team. But for sales managers, goals are based on how well the people they're managing produce. If the sales manager's team succeeds, she succeeds. This can be an uncomfortable feeling—particularly for former salespeople, who tend to like being in control of every situation.

When you see a member of your team making a glaring mistake, the urge to sweep her to the side and take over will be almost irresistible, but you have to resist the urge and let her learn from her own mistakes. Similarly, you can't rescue your salespeople from the results of their errors. The only way they'll become better salespeople is if you give them the chance to fall on their faces and then pick themselves up again.

ARE YOU A COMPANY PERSON?

One of a sales manager's most important tasks is conveying information from upper management to the sales team and back. Any time there's a change in the compensation plan, a new product, or a territory revision, the sales manager has to explain it to the sales team. But just explaining is not enough—he has to essentially sell them on the changes. If the team doesn't like or accept management's policies, there will be serious trouble, and it's up to the sales manager to keep that from happening.

Middle Management

Sales managers are almost inevitably middle managers. That means they're caught between the people who report to them and the upper levels of management. Balancing the needs of both sides can be quite a challenge.

CAN YOU HANDLE (LOTS OF) MEETINGS?

Most salespeople hate sales meetings, but guess what: sales managers have to attend a *lot* of them. Not only does a sales manager run the regular sales meetings, but he also has one-on-one meetings with individual team members, meetings with marketing, meetings with upper management, etc.

CAN YOU SEE THE BIG PICTURE?

A salesperson is responsible for her own quota and accounts. But sales managers have to juggle the whole team's needs. This can be a real problem when several salespeople need help at once. Sales managers are also often responsible for setting quotas, drawing up sales plans, and making forecasts, all of which require analytical thinking and the ability to stay organized.

ARE YOU THICK-SKINNED?

When a salesperson is having difficulties, he's likely to become emotional. That's why it's vital to keep your own emotions under control. You need to let him vent without taking what he says personally. Once he's released some of his frustration, you can then direct him to a solution. But if you get upset and frustrated yourself, you'll just make it more difficult for him to recover. You'll probably face other troublesome situations, from firing a salesperson who isn't performing to dealing with a hostile customer who insists on speaking with the manager, and in each of these encounters maintaining your control will help you to find a solution.

HOW TO COACH SALESPEOPLE

Guide, Don't Ride

Coaching your sales team is one of the most important of sales management tasks. It's by coaching that you and your salespeople can figure out which of their skills and processes need work, and come up with a plan for improving them. It's also one of the most challenging aspects of sales management for former salespeople, since people who do well in sales generally aren't natural coaches.

When something goes wrong, it's often easier for an outsider to figure out the cause. For example, a salesperson who's struggling to make appointments might not realize that her script has gone stale and she's reading it like a robot. As her sales manager, you're ideally placed to both identify the problem and to help her fix it.

Effective sales coaching follows a four-step process. First, you sit down with a salesperson to review her recent performance and identify any weak areas. Second, the two of you figure out a plan for fixing those problem areas. Third, you both commit to carrying out each step of this plan over a certain time frame. Finally, you schedule a meeting at the end of said time frame to see if the plan has helped the salesperson to improve her performance and to discuss the next steps.

Before you can review the salesperson's performance, you'll need to have accurate metrics for that salesperson. Without hard data on which sales activities she's doing and what results she's getting from them, you won't be able to tell why she's doing worse—or better—this month than she did in the last one.

Looking at those sales metrics enables you to narrow down which stage of the sales process is causing her problems. For example, if she's making plenty of cold calls and converting a decent percentage of them to appointments, and her total number of closed sales is low, then there's either a problem with her sales presentation or with her closing. Ask her to demonstrate both her sales pitch and her favorite closing method to you (preferably as part of a role-play exercise) or shadow her on a couple of appointments, and you should soon be able to figure out which one is the problem.

Once you know what the problem is, it's time for you to come up with a way to fix it. This is where many sales managers make the mistake of going into "boss mode" and telling the salesperson what she's going to do to fix it, instead of helping her work out the answer herself.

Put yourself back into a salesperson's mindset for moment. If you order a prospect to buy your product and say it will solve his problem, the prospect will not only say no; he'll also think you're a total jerk. Your salesperson won't react in quite this way because you are, after all, her boss—but she'll resent being ordered around, especially about an issue like her poor performance. So instead of just telling her how to solve the problem, encourage your salesperson to come up with an answer herself and then validate her answer. Because she came up with it herself, the salesperson will have a sense of ownership about her plan and will be much more motivated to stick to it.

The Socratic Method

The ancient Greek philosopher Socrates taught his students by asking questions and encouraging them to figure out the answers. This approach is still one of the most respected teaching methods today, and it's a great format to use for coaching salespeople.

Step three is the one that sales managers are most likely to skip, which is unfortunate because it's an important part of the process. Without a commitment and a series of clearly defined steps, including a completion date for each stage, your plan will keep getting pushed aside in favor of more urgent tasks. As a result, the salesperson will never see an improvement in that problem area, and you'll end up having exactly the same discussion next month.

For the final step you'll want to schedule a one-on-one meeting to discuss how well the plan worked, how difficult it was to carry out, and whether you need to keep trying the same plan, try something new, or declare this issue resolved. For more complex problems, you might want to schedule several brief meetings at different stages of the plan to track the salesperson's progress.

During the final meeting it's important for you and the salesperson to come to an agreement on whether or not the plan worked well, and if it didn't, what went wrong. It's also important for you to recognize clearly and loudly any progress that the salesperson made in improving her numbers. Salespeople thrive on recognition, and will be far more motivated to keep working on the problem and to tackle other problems in the future if you're generous with the praise they've earned.

While it's important to spend time with each member of your sales team, realistically most of your time will be spent with the salespeople who are having the most trouble meeting their goals. Still, you've got to make sure that each member of your team gets at least one coaching session with you per month. Even the best performers have room for improvement, and the salespeople in the middle of the pack can be encouraged to move up.

COMMON SALES MANAGEMENT CHALLENGES

How to Hurdle Them

Sales managers tend to encounter the same basic problems in every company they work for. Most businesses share at least some of these issues, so knowing how to deal with them can help a sales manager resolve a problem situation.

LITTLE OR NO TRAINING

Executives often figure that promoting the top seller on the sales team into a leadership position means they don't need to provide sales management training. Unfortunately, sales training isn't the same as sales *management* training. Managing well requires a whole different set of people skills than selling, although someone who's mastered sales will likely get the hang of it quickly once he understands the difference between the two.

How to Deal

If your company has placed you in a sales management role without offering any management training at all, you'll need to take matters into your own hands. Start by doing some research to identify a suitable course, then put in a request with your boss to have the company send you to that course. If the company refuses to pay for it, you may have to take care of the costs on your own, but it will be time and money well spent if it helps you to perform your job better and more easily.

THE WRONG RESPONSIBILITIES

Many jobs with the title of "sales manager" are actually more along the lines of sales management plus marketing management plus administrative management. The sales manager gets all the vaguely sales-related scut work handed to her and ends up spending her time coordinating campaigns with other departments, making presentations to upper management, doing paperwork, and writing reports instead of actually managing the sales team.

How to Deal

If you find yourself in this situation, your best recourse is to calculate how much time you spend on various tasks and then present that information to your boss (including charts and graphs if possible). Explain that you need to refocus the position to concentrate more on sales management responsibilities. Hiring an administrative assistant to handle the more tedious tasks may be all that's necessary to solve the problem.

Forget the TPS Reports

The three most crucial sales management tasks are sales planning, coaching your salespeople, and helping out with stalled deals and similar problems. If you just don't have time to do all your assigned tasks, do those three first and cram in whatever else you can manage.

NO FREEDOM TO ACT

Like most middle managers, sales managers are responsible for managing their sales teams but report to higher-level managers themselves. This typical middle management structure means that sales managers may need to get approval from upper management before they can do certain tasks that are intrinsic to the job.

For example, if a salesperson on the team is failing because he needs more training, has a poor territory assignment, or is just not doing the job, the sales manager may have to go through a long, drawn-out approval process before he can act to resolve the problem—even when he knows exactly how to fix the problem. Meanwhile the salesperson's poor performance is hurting the team's overall standing and lowering the manager's numbers.

How to Deal

Developing some "action plans" and getting your boss's approval for them in advance can help to speed up resolution during a crisis. If you already have executive approval for a basic sales training program, all you need is permission to use the plan as necessary. You'll likely also need to request a budget to fund such programs; the smaller the budget you request, the more likely you are to get approval, so try to work out the cheapest possible way to fix common sales problems.

LACK OF INFORMATION

Sales managers know what leads the sales team gets, and they are most definitely aware of how many deals their salespeople close and how close they are to meeting their quotas. But what happens in between acquiring a lead list and closing the sale is often shrouded in a fog of mystery. Without a clear understanding of the process an individual salesperson uses, sales managers will have trouble figuring out the problem if that person's production drops. And it's not just salespeople who withhold information; upper management may fail to keep you posted about upcoming changes to compensation plans, quota structures, and the like.

How to Deal

A good customer relationship management (CRM) system can be helpful for tracking activities...as long as the salespeople are conscientious about keeping their records updated as each sale progresses. Another possibility is to set activity goals for the sales team. For instance, each salesperson might be responsible for completing one hundred cold calls and five appointments each week, with the calls and appointments logged on paper and given to the sales manager every Friday. Finally, regular coaching is a good way to catch small problems before they become big ones.

Staying informed of upper management's plans is a bit more of a challenge. Try to cultivate a "mole," someone in executive country who can informally keep you updated about what's in the works. Failing that, get friendly with a few administrative assistants of those executives. Assistants are likely to be far more informed than you are and usually won't mind sharing tidbits of information in exchange for your gratitude and the occasional free lunch.

HOW TO HELP YOUR TEAM SUCCEED

Leading Your Salespeople to the Top

Sales is a high-stress job. The more support you can give your salespeople, the easier it will be for them to become successful. And since your compensation is tied to how well your sales team produces, you'll be amply rewarded for helping them out. In particular watch out for the four most common areas where salespeople tend to struggle.

LACK OF CONFIDENCE

Salespeople have to deal with rejection on a daily (and sometimes hourly) basis. This can drain the energy of even the most experienced salesperson after a while, while new salespeople often have trouble coping with it from the beginning. A lack of confidence often shows itself in salespeople through behaviors like avoiding making calls; making negative assertions, such as "People just aren't interested in our products"; and spending as much time as they can on non-sales activities.

Although you can't give your salespeople a gift of self-confidence, you can help them to create it on their own. Schedule a coaching session with the struggling salesperson and use it to brainstorm a few ideas that she can use to improve her sales. If your salespeople develop confidence in your recommendations and strategies, they'll feel more optimistic about the results of their sales activities—which in turn will make them more likely to succeed. And this success will help build their confidence in themselves.

DEPENDENCE ON YOU

Of course, it's possible for the approach described previously to backfire. Your salespeople might be so impressed by your awe-inspiring wisdom that they're reluctant to do anything on their own. Such salespeople may ask you to listen in on calls or come with them on appointments on a regular basis, or they might regularly need you to close their sales for them.

Helping out occasionally with a difficult prospect is fine, but it's not okay for your salespeople to expect you to do all the selling for them or to hold their hands throughout every potentially challenging situation. If you see a pattern of dependence developing, it's time to draw back and say, "I think you should handle this one." Once they've successfully completed a few sales on their own, your salespeople will be feeling much more capable.

BURNOUT

Every so often salespeople may find themselves in an emotional rut. They just aren't feeling motivated and have difficulty doing anything beyond the bare minimum. The easiest way to identify this problem is simply to listen to a salesperson interacting with customers and prospects. A burned-out salesperson will do as little as possible and will usually demonstrate a lack of energy in his tone of voice and body language.

The best and most effective way to get a salesperson out of this kind of rut is to have him try something entirely new. Give him a completely new cold calling script, or, even better, have him write a brand-new script himself. Another option is to have him try a sales channel he's never used before, such as social media. If nothing else works, you might just want to send him home on vacation for a week or two to recover from the stress of the job.

Firing Salespeople

Sometimes a salesperson gets burned out beyond recovery. At that point it's time to ease him out of sales and into a new career. If you approach the subject kindly, you may convince the salesperson to quit. Otherwise, you'll have to fire him yourself—an unpleasant but necessary solution.

FRUSTRATION

A salesperson who's really having trouble hitting a tough quota or who's been in a sales slump for a while will probably get frustrated. This is not unlike a salesperson who's burned out or lacking confidence, but instead of going limp, the frustrated salesperson gets angry. He may demonstrate a hostile edge in his interactions with other people, even in sales situations. The frustrated salesperson is also likely to take rejection personally, whether it's a prospect who hangs up on him during a cold call or you making helpful suggestions.

You can aid the frustrated salesperson by giving him an opportunity to vent. Schedule a one-on-one meeting and ask him to talk to you about what he's been going through. It may take some nudging on your part for him to feel safe enough to talk freely, so be patient. Once he's had a chance to rant a little about everything that's been going wrong, he'll feel a lot better. At that point you can discuss his goals with him and jointly develop a plan that will get him to those goals. Be sure to set milestones along the route to his goal and set up some type of reward each time he reaches one. Enabling him to follow a clearly defined pathway toward his goal should relieve your salesperson of much of his frustration, especially once he's achieved a few successes.

INDEX

ABOUT THE AUTHOR

Wendy Connick's first sales position was a summer job selling vacuum cleaners door-to-door. Eventually she switched over to the informational side of sales and began writing and managing all content on the Sales site for About.com (now *Dotdash*). She has also written for the National Association of Sales Professionals blog. As a professional writer, Wendy now focuses on helping other people master the art of selling and other crucial life skills.

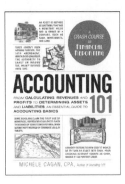